"Dudley Hall's ability to make eternal realities
ter (not to mention meat and potatoes, as we
to experience! I'm thrilled to see the publica
when Dudley talks about grace, you really do find out how it works."

JACK W. HAYFORD
FOUNDER AND PRESIDENT, KING'S COLLEGE AND SEMINARY,
LOS ANGELES, CALIFORNIA

"I am happy to recommend this second edition of *Grace Works.* It is a profound book revealing the subtle trap of pharisaic religion and the reasons why so many well-meaning and vibrant believers fall into it. With vivid illustrations and simple language, one of America's most extraordinary teachers shows the way to live in the joy of grace-filled intimacy with the Lord."

DR. JACK DEERE
DEAN OF THE WAGNER LEADERSHIP INSTITUTE,
COLORADO SPRINGS, COLORADO

"Grace does work! How sad that it is so often misunderstood and misapplied. We're not talking about something cheap. We're talking about God's great gift at an indescribable price. Through His marvelous provision, we can receive abundantly beyond anything we ever imagined, and we don't have to earn it. The fact is, when true grace is received, there will be both a divine enabling and an irresistible urging to release what we have received. Dudley Hall makes this reality unmistakably clear."

JAMES ROBISON
FOUNDER AND PRESIDENT, LIFE OUTREACH INTERNATIONAL,
FORT WORTH, TEXAS

"Grace is so absolutely incredible, and law and works so ever present in our minds and hearts as a way to please God, that constant reminders are necessary. *Grace Works* is a powerful, easy-to-read reminder of the truth about grace, the grace that works in us for the glory of God. There is no one I know who consistently communicates the truths of God more simply and clearly than Dudley. A must reminder for all of us who are easily drawn back into the works trap."

PETER LORD
AUTHOR AND POPULAR CONFERENCE SPEAKER

"Must reading for the weary Christian pilgrim."

DENNIS PEACOCKE

STRATEGIC CHRISTIAN SERVICES, SANTA ROSA, CALIFORNIA

"Many in ministry have labored long in the "brick-making" business. Dudley Hall, through solid biblical interpretation, wonderful illustrations, and reasoned explanation, has called us from a brick-making mentality to a kingdom-building destiny. To all who are tired of being disillusioned by trying to fulfill unrealistic, unbiblical, and irrational expectations…rejoice! This book will serve as a map out of that religious jungle."

DR. DOUG WHITE

SENIOR PASTOR, RESTORATION CHURCH, EULESS, TEXAS

"Dudley Hall has once again put the amazing back into grace. With the skilled precision of a smart bomb, *Grace Works* destroys the futile efforts of performance and leaves the reader resting in the sufficiency of Christ."

NORM WILLIS

AUTHOR AND SENIOR PASTOR, CHRIST CHURCH KIRKLAND, KIRKLAND, WASHINGTON

GRACE WORKS

LETTING GOD RESCUE YOU FROM EMPTY RELIGION

Multnomah® Publishers *Sisters, Oregon*

DUDLEY HALL

GRACE WORKS

published by Multnomah Publishers, Inc.

International Standard Book Number: 1-57673-575-3

Cover photograph by: Lorenz Avelar/Direct Stock Inc.
Cover design by: Chris Gilbert

Printed in the United States of America

FOR INFORMATION:
Multnomah Publishers, Inc.,
Post Office Box 1720
Sisters, Oregon 97759

00 01 02 03 04 05 06 — 10 9 8 7 6 5 4 3 2 1 0

Dedication

I dedicate this book to my family. It is through each of them that I have come to experience the true grace of God. Betsy, my wife, is truly God's perfect gift to me. She comforts and confronts with equal graciousness and challenges me to be real at all cost. Her willingness to give all constantly moves me toward Jesus. David, our firstborn, has so obviously been God's possession that to rear him as our son has been God's special favor to us. While in my seminary studies I was arrested by the beauty of the greek word CHARIS, which we translate "grace." I said then, "If I ever have a daughter, I would like her name to be Charis." God blessed Betsy and me with a daughter and we named her Karis (to get the correct pronunciation in English we used "K" instead of "Ch"). She is a constant reminder to us of God's delight in goodness, of his every ready desire to pour himself out to us. She has brought immeasurable delight into our lives.

These three have been God's favorite channels of grace to me. I am forever grateful for their love. My prayer is that we all will always walk in God's grace.

CONTENTS

INTRODUCTION

The Good News Gospel

THE GOSPEL HAS TAKEN a bad rap!

More often than not, what is proclaimed as gospel is just another challenge to "do better." Try harder! Pray longer! Be more committed! Love deeper! Stop sinning! Be good! Be happy!

All of these commands come as bad news to people who are trapped by their own guilt-ridden, inadequate lives. People who have tried to do better but failed. People who are already over-committed and trapped by sin and well aware that they fall far short of good. People who have tried and tried but just can't manage to be truly, deeply happy.

No wonder the church has failed to connect with so many people out there! The hurting masses of the world are seeking a cure for their ills and solutions for their problems. And too often, the church has promised them everything but given them next to nothing in the name of gospel. Just more expectations to fulfill, more rules to keep, more activities to maintain, more work to do. The result has been a trail of discouragement and disillusionment. It's caused a lot of people to reject the church entirely.

And the tragedy is that this "do better" mentality and the lifestyle it spawns is light years removed from the kind of life Jesus demonstrated. Jesus was never the victim of his environment. He chose the course he would take, even the death he would die. He was never bound by bitterness, hatred, lust, fear, or jealousy. He was never anxious about his security nor worried about his position. He never resorted to manipulation or coercion to get his way. He healed the sick, cast out demons, raised the dead, stilled the storms, gave sight to the blind, and loved everybody everywhere. He was known as a friend of sinners. Prostitutes and criminals did not feel condemned in his presence. He could laugh at the comedy in life and cry over the deception that blinded men to life's beauty. And even when his contemporaries rejected him, Jesus lived with no self-rejection. His intimacy with his heavenly Father was enough. He could even face the devil personally and not fail because he trusted the identity and acceptance his Father had given him.

What a life! Who wouldn't want the kind of life that was never at the mercy of circumstances and always one step ahead of all foes?

But that life is not what people have rejected, of course. They've rejected the pitiful substitute bearing the name "religion"—that complex, complicated system of theological dogmas and behavioral requirements the polluted church has offered. It's erroneously been called gospel... "good news." And the understandable response has been, "If that's good news, I'm sunk. No thank you." Roy Hession, a noted author and respected evangelist from Great Britain, often said, "I've heard many sermons. Most of them are good advice, but not many are good news."

And yet God does have a "good news" message for the world and for the believer, and it's just the opposite of "do better." The good news God sends us through Jesus Christ is the message of *grace*. It's the liberating message of "This is what I want to do for you—not because you've done better or tried harder or stopped sinning, but because you're my child, and I love you!"

What specifically does the Father offer? It's the gift of

"eternal life"—life with the eternal quality of God in it. It exists in time and space, but it has the ability to transcend human limitations and explore the vastness of the spiritual world. And it comes through a personal relationship with God himself.

Think of a joyous father who brings home a new car for his sixteen-year-old daughter. She jumps up and down in excitement, but inside feels a sense of uncertainty. She has never seen a car like this. It has so many buttons, switches, and levers! How will she ever make it work? But her father lovingly and willingly demonstrates the car for her. He drives it around the block, putting it through its paces as she watches. She can't believe all the things it will do!

The father then gives her the keys and the title. It's her car now. But he still doesn't leave her. He gets in beside her and patiently shows her how to carry out every aspect of its operation. And he stays with her, continuing to reveal new and exciting capabilities she never imagined possible.

That's the kind of love and freedom and excitement contained in the authentic gospel message. It's a gift freely given, a gift of grace.

Instead of chiding, "Do better," grace whispers, "I want to do this *for* you." Instead of urging, "try harder," grace murmurs, "I've done the hard work for you. Rest in me and work in my power. And remember: I love you no matter what."

Grace is a message of unconditional love from the Father of the universe. It's the free offer of eternal life. And we can experience it all in the gritty now as well as in the sweet by and by.

That's the real gospel—and it's really good news! So join me while I explore the full and life-giving implications of the gospel of grace.

PART ONE

The Grace of Who I Am

Therefore if any man is in Christ, he is a new creature; the old things passed away; behold, new things have come. **2 Corinthians 5:17**

CHAPTER

1 The "Oughteries"

SEVERAL YEARS AGO I was interviewed on a religious TV program and afterward had lunch with the host. While we were awaiting on our Caesar salad, I asked him, "Tell me your story. When did you come to know Jesus personally?"

The show host eagerly related that he had made his profession of faith as a young boy, but had drifted away for sixteen years of rebellion before coming to know the fullness of the life of Jesus Christ. He told how a well-known minister had loved him and prayed with him as he experienced a newfound forgiveness and joy in life.

He then turned to me: "Tell me your story."

Thinking about the parallels of our lives, I heard myself saying, "I, too, made an early commitment to God. But I spent several years in *religion* before coming to embrace the freedom of Jesus' life."

The interesting thing is that the quality of our "before" lifestyles—his in rebellion and mine in religion—was not all that different! Neither of us had real joy.

In some ways, in fact, my new friend's rebellious lifestyle seemed preferable to my religious one. At least he knew he was wrong. I thought I was doing what God wanted. And he experienced some of the world's best offerings that were fun for awhile, while I tried to gain satisfaction with my regimens and disciplines, telling myself that when I finally got to heaven I would be glad I had rejected the sinful ways of the world.

I lived a behaviorly pure life. Except for "minor" infractions, I restrained from bad-boy behavior. My selfish desires were as evil as anyone's, but I refrained from acting on them most of the time. When I failed, I spent a considerable amount of time paying for my failure with an appropriate amount of guilt. My definition of holiness was one of external deeds and church-related activities. I viewed "being good" more in terms of what to avoid than what to do.

But this was not a quality lifestyle, and it certainly did not deserve to be exported. It was not attractive to the person next door, much less to the "heathen in foreign lands."

Even more important, it was not the life that Jesus came to bring me. It was not a gospel lifestyle.

Jesus himself made that clear in a wonderful story recorded in the fifteenth chapter of Luke. This story about a father and his two sons is one of the best-known stories in the Bible. It's usually called "The Parable of the Prodigal Son," but that title is a little misleading. For while the younger son—the so-called "Prodigal" gets most of the attention from the casual Bible reader, the real emphasis of the story is on the *second* boy. It could just as easily be called "The Parable of the Older Brother."

THE SECOND SON'S STORY

Jesus, remember, was speaking to the religious leaders of his day, who were not at all happy about Jesus' kindness to the nonreligious. In the minds of these religious people, anyone who rejected "holiness" deserved to be punished and certainly couldn't expect to be treated the same way after the rebellion as they had before it.

The religious leaders just couldn't swallow Jesus' emphasis

on forgiving sinners and restoring them to non-guilty status. So Jesus told this story to reveal their stupidity and blindness.

You remember how the story starts out: The younger son of a wealthy father asks for his inheritance, and the father complies with his request. The boy then goes his own way and spends every bit of his inheritance "making merry" in the far country. Finally, hungry and degraded, he decides to go home and throw himself on his father's mercy. He muses, "Even my father's hired servants have it better than I." So he comes home willing to be a servant. But his father, overjoyed at his homecoming, puts a robe on his back, a ring on his finger, shoes on his feet... and throws a feast to celebrate his return.

Meanwhile, the older son hears the noise of the celebration and comes to see what is going on. When told that his brother is home and is welcome, he pitches a fit. And his mistaken concept of what pleases his father is revealed by three statements he makes. In my mind, these statements summarize the faulty ideas that keep a lot of us trapped in religion instead of living full, free lives in Jesus:

"Look What I've Done for You!" First, the older brother whines, "All these years I have served thee." He was living under the impression that service is the key to pleasing the father.

I once heard Peter Lord, pastor of Park Avenue Baptist Church in Titusville, Florida, and my longtime friend, say, "Wouldn't it be awful to spend all your life trying to make God an apple pie, only to die and discover he never liked apple pie?" It wasn't service for which we were created. It was and is *fellowship*. The Father likes to share life with his children. He is pleased when those children receive his life and enjoy it.

When our son was about nine years old, he and I had a confrontation one day about his procrastination in doing some yard work. I picked up the paddle (he remembers it as a ten-foot two-by-four!), and he took off. Out the back door and down the street he ran. I ran after him. He wisely ascertained that he was about to be caught and stopped. Then, in a last-ditch effort to save himself and gain some pity, he pleaded, "The only reason you had me was so I could work for you."

That ridiculous plea struck me as so funny that I dropped the paddle and fell to the ground laughing. (He now says that God gave him a supernatural word of wisdom in order to save his life!)

We had him for the work he would do? How ridiculous! While laughing, I began calculating how much I had invested in that boy thus far. A hospital bill of three thousand dollars at birth. Medical and dental bills of at least ten thousand since that time. At least ten thousand dollars in clothing expense. Over eight thousand for food and entertainment . . .

I had been ripped off! I had spent at least thirty thousand dollars to get my lawn mowed a few times!

Those who believe that service is the key to pleasing God will keep careful records of their service. They may even be found using their service record to gain leverage in bargaining with God for some desired blessing.

But Jesus has news for them. What they have done for God is nothing when compared to the immeasurable value of what God has done for them!

Keeping the Rules and Missing the Party. Second, the older son says, "I never transgressed thy commandment at any time." He was assuming that pleasing the father is essentially a matter of keeping the outward rules. And because of that mistaken assumption, he was still standing outside the party, refusing to enjoy the full life of fellowship offered by the father.

The Pharisees were champions at keeping rules. But Jesus, instead of praising them, just accused them of being full of corruption and deception.

The self-righteousness of those who define life in terms of outward rules, restrictions, and regulations is unbearable. They aren't having any fun, and they won't allow you to have any, either. If you don't live up to their expectations, you must be punished by rejection and criticism, at the very least.

Blind and Miserable. The older son's third statement was, "You never gave me a kid [a goat] that I might make merry with my friends." He had been living with a definite unsatisfied desire—he had always wanted a kid to barbecue. His life has been devoid of joy because he can't have his kid and his party.

The father seems shocked by that response. "Look at all the kids on our farm. There are thousands. They all belong to you. All that is mine is thine."

What blindness! It is the same blindness of the younger son. Neither could see what was theirs in the father's house.

One left seeking, only to return when he realized what was his in his father and began to value it. The other remained but couldn't see what he possessed, either. The blindness of rebellion or religion will produce the same inferior-quality lifestyle.

JESUS AND THE "OUGHTERIES"

Someone once told me he knew why so many Christians look so miserable. "They are all suffering from hardening of the 'oughteries.' They never feel they have done as much as they ought to have done."

That was exactly what the older brother's problem was. It was also the affliction of a woman I met while serving as guest speaker at a central Texas church some time back. I arrived at the church early and waited in the foyer. A woman came in and sat down in the same area while we waited for someone to open the doors to the main auditorium.

Making conversation, I asked, "Do you attend church here?"

"Not as much as I ought to," she replied sheepishly.

Realizing she felt examined, I tried to relieve the pressure by saying, "Well, isn't it wonderful to go to church because you want to rather than because you ought to?"

"Yeah, but I don't want to as much as I ought to."

What a trap the oughteries are! You can never do enough.

If you pray for two hours, you should have prayed more, or you should have been more serious. If you fasted for one week you should have fasted longer. Just think of what you could have accomplished if you hadn't quit so soon!

But Jesus didn't live with the oughteries. He *wanted* to do the will of his father. He lived out of the inner motivation of the heart in a vital relationship with a living God.

In fact, when Jesus was only twelve, he gave his parents a good scare because, when they started for home after a temple visit, he stayed behind, discussing his Father's business with the religious leaders of the day. He was so caught up with being there that he completely forgot about his family. There was no "I ought to be here to please God."

On another occasion, Jesus was traveling through Samaria on his way to Galilee. He had stopped at a well at Sychar to rest while his disciples went into town to get some food. A needy woman with a bad reputation came to the well at midday to fetch water and to escape the menacing looks and catty remarks of the town's women. Jesus took enough time to get involved in that woman's life and to offer her the life of God. As a result, she ran back into town and evangelized the whole area. And this all happened while Jesus was "off duty"—while he was resting.

The disciples came back with food, expecting him to be famished and ready to eat. But Jesus wasn't hungry. "I have meat to eat that you don't know about," he told them. They couldn't understand. Who had brought Jesus food? They had been to town as quickly as possible; who could have arrived before them?

"It is my meat to do the will of my Father," Jesus revealed. In other words, "I would rather do the will of God than eat." No oughteries here. Jesus was energized by doing the will of God. And it was not the draining work of religion that he was talking about. He didn't gripe about being called on to work when he needed to be resting. He was simply enjoying the life of God being lived out in the flesh. That same life is given to believers when they receive the grace of God in Jesus Christ.

NO "OUGHTERIES," JUST OPPORTUNITIES

Much of Jesus' time on earth was spent praying. Yet the emphasis in his prayer life was not posture or platitudes, but fellowship. Certainly he spent whole nights in prayer. But I get the distinct impression that these were not planned prayer meetings. These were times of unparalleled communion with the Father. To Jesus, this fellowship was obviously better than sleep. He was hearing the heart of God himself, tapping into the wisdom of the universe. In these times of communion he could see the divine perspective... life from God's point of view. Sleep couldn't hold a candle to that kind of joy!

Even when Jesus was tempted by Satan himself in the wilderness, he was unswayed by the "oughteries." He had heard the voice of the Father at his baptism saying, "This is my beloved Son in whom I am well pleased." And then he had immediately been led by the Spirit into the wilderness to be tempted. The first recorded temptation was this: "If you are the Son of God, prove it by turning these stones into bread." But Jesus was resting in the reality of God's word to him and obviously felt no need to prove his identity. The word he gives us through "The Parable of the Older Brother" is that *we* don't have to prove anything, either.

What a relief for believers! You don't have to prove you are somebody by what you do. God alone gives you your identity and that's settled, regardless of what you do. There are no "oughteries" in the life of grace, just plenty of opportunities to experience the very life of God. You don't have to spend your life examining yourself and measuring yourself by some external definition of good. Your worthiness is not dependent upon how well you perform. You were paid for with God's only begotten Son. You are valuable. You can be free to act out of your wholeness rather than your sickness.

God has offered a lifestyle in Jesus that actually allows you to do what you want. But first he instructs you as to who you really are—a chosen child of the living God. Forgiven totally, accepted fully, a living container of marvelous grace!

CHAPTER 2

The "Do to Be" Tree

"THERE WERE TWO TREES in the garden." That simple statement seems so innocuous, so unimportant. But therein lies the choice that determines the quality of life we experience.

I'm referring, of course, to the two trees that grew in the middle of the Garden of Eden: the "tree of life" and the second—forbidden—"tree of the knowledge of good and evil" (Gn 2:9). According to the Genesis account, Adam and Eve chose the latter, sealing their doom and laying the pattern for centuries of humans to come.

Rick Joyner, in his masterful study of that fateful choice, says the two trees are a picture of the eternal choice we must make —the choice of whether to embrace a life of *relationship with God* or one of *independence from God.*[1]

THE "DO TO BE" MINDSET

The "tree of the knowledge of good and evil" offers men and women a chance to go it alone—to obtain and achieve for themselves the necessary elements for "the good life." Satan uses that tree to solidify his big lie, "You have to *do* to *be:* If you

1. Rick Joyner, *There Were Two Trees in the Garden,* (Charlotte, N.C.: Morningstar Publications, 1986).

will eat, you will be like God." Once the fruit from that tree is eaten, humanity is never released from the need to perform until we die. We are blinded by the need to "do something." We not only become *performers,* but judges of *performance*—our own and others'.

There are some terrible pitfalls in the "do to be" mentality.

First, when we succeed in doing something right, we expect God to be pleased and to bless us as a result. Then, if it doesn't happen, we are terribly disillusioned. We also tend to develop pride in accomplishment.

Second, we invariably judge ourselves worthless if we fail. After all, failing at a task must mean I am a *failure.* Identity is determined by behavior, isn't it?

But this entire way of thinking is contrary to the way God planned life to be. The Tower of Babel is an eternal monument to the inability of humankind to reach God through our own efforts. I'm almost certain there was a banner draped over the work area: "If it is to be, it is up to me." We can learn from that historical disaster that God is not impressed with people who attempt to reach him through their own efforts in order to make a name for themselves. He doesn't accept the "do to be" philosophy of life.

THE "WHO I AM" ALTERNATIVE

So, what's the alternative? It's the mindset that begins with essence, not performance; who I am, not what I do. And "who I am" begins with who I was created to be—a person living in intimate communion with God. That's why the "tree of life" represents the choice of *relationship* with God.

Although the first Adam chose the wrong tree and infected all men with "performance-itis," the "last Adam"—Jesus—chose this second tree. And his life is the model of life at its best.

Jesus did nothing of public significance before he was thirty years of age except for his brief encounter with the religious leaders in the temple at age twelve. At the inauguration of his public ministry, before Jesus had performed any miracles or preached any sermons, God the Father stated Jesus' identity. Jesus was the Son of God, and God was already pleased with him—without a performance of any kind.

It was this confidence in his relationship and his identity in the Father that gave Jesus the fortitude to stand against the devil, withstand rejection from friends, and suffer unjustly. When accused of being demon-possessed, for example, he did not fall prey to defensiveness and cry in his own behalf, "I am not. I'll have you know I am the Son of God." He needed no defense. He knew who he was. And everything he did grew out of that basic confidence.

THE FREEDOM OF BEING WHO YOU ARE

Since Jesus, the last Adam, illustrates the lifestyle that comes from the tree of life, we can observe in him a wonderfully liberating truth: Our lives are most full and satisfying when *being* defines *doing*.

Nature defines character. Who we are determines what we do.

This "be to do" truth is reflected in the nature of all physical life. Species determine characteristics. Biological life is classified into distinct phyla based on this immutable fact.

Travel with me for a moment into the world of imagination to see this wonderful truth illustrated. A few years ago I went to the kennel in my yard to visit with my three dogs: Gus, Snow, and Scratch. Scratch was in the pits. Depression is too mild a word to describe his state; he was talking of suicide.

Here was the situation: Gus, the oldest dog in the kennel, had used his position to deceive poor ol' Scratch. He had told Scratch that he was a cat—and Scratch had believed it. Trying to be a good cat, Scratch had begun studying cat behavior and trying to act like a cat. But he wasn't very good at it. He tried to meow, but failed. He attempted to climb trees, but failed at that as well. He hated cat food and couldn't purr.

A failure! That was Scratch's final assessment of himself. He didn't deserve to live. He was taking up space that some good cat could occupy, eating food that some worthy cat should eat. Suicide was the honorable thing to do. But before he took that final out, he asked me for help.

"I can help you," I told Scratch.

"Really?" he prayed. "Please, anything. Put me on the couch. Cast out demons. Anything!"

"You got yourself into this mess," I said, "by believing a lie. You can get yourself out by believing the truth. You aren't a cat. You are a dog. Go be yourself."

Dogs like to bark. And strangely enough, they are equipped to bark. Dogs like to dig, and they have that capability. Scratch was a bird dog. This particular species has both the desire and ability to hunt quail. In the same way, cats meow. They like to meow. They're good at it. And birds fly. Fish swim.

You get the point. When God creates a species, he gives it the desire and ability to do what he intended it to do.

Now, here's another important consideration. Christians are a "new creature"—a "new species" (2 Cor 5:17). We have the very life of Christ in us. There has never been another species like the one created when God's Spirit becomes one with a human being's spirit. And this form of life has the capability and desire to live the same way Jesus lived on earth.

Our trouble comes when, like Scratch, we choose a course of action contrary to our nature. When dogs try to act like cats, they are contradicting their nature. When birds try to act like fish, they are miserable. And when Christians try to act like anything other than the new creation they are, they become paralyzed, because they have violated their nature. True freedom comes from choosing actions that are consistent with your nature.

ALL WE WERE MEANT TO BE

Embracing this perspective opens our eyes to the beauty of God's commands. God knows our true nature and desires for us to discover it. So each command is a challenge to discover abilities yet untapped.

He often commands things that are beyond human potential. For instance, he says, "Love your enemies." I have enough trouble loving my friends, even my spiritual family. If this command is something I must fulfill on my own to gain God's blessing and pleasure, I'm in deep trouble. But along with this command I am given the *love* to accomplish it. And I've discovered an aspect of eternal life I hadn't known before.

You might remember the man with the withered hand who was confronted by Jesus. "Stretch out your hand," demanded Jesus (Mk 3:5).

What a cruel thing to say to a man who obviously couldn't use his hand. The man could have argued, "Please ask me to do something I am able to do. Capitalize on my strengths and overlook my liabilities. I can do many things for you if you will but let me perform. Why, look at my walking. There is nothing wrong with my feet. I can talk for you; there is nothing wrong with my mouth."

But Jesus wasn't interested in what the man could do for him. He wanted to do something for the man. He wanted the man to experience a new kind of life... eternal life. But that kind of life can only be experienced by faith.

It is no different when he commands us to do the impossible. He is trying to help us discover that we have a quality of life greater than we can imagine. Difficulties take on a different value when seen from the perspective of eternal life. Since our Father knows what he has placed within us and we do not, he is constantly leading us into situations where our real capabilities are revealed.

At the risk of boring you with another "dog story," let me tell you about training bird dog puppies. They are so cute when they're little, but they don't have a clue as to who they are or what they are on earth for. As their trainer, it is my job to help them discover their destiny. Their Creator has already done the difficult part; he made them with all the necessary equipment to get the job done.

Here is the scene: I take a young dog into the field and let him run. He simply enjoys being a dog. He chases butterflies, smells the flowers, jumps the ditches, sniffs around. But I have a plan. I have planted some live birds in the corner of the field. I slowly guide him around to a position downwind of the birds. As the scent of those birds begins to penetrate his cute little nostrils, something wonderful and strange begins to take place. He immediately stops. He goes rigid, and he lifts his right front paw. He has just pointed his first bird. He didn't know he could do that. It just happened when he was exposed to the right conditions. And I love to see it happen.

In the same sense, I get a kick out of taking people onto the streets to minister. Most go hesitantly. They feel inadequate. They are intimidated. I try to take the pressure of performance off by saying, "You don't have to witness. No one is going to ask you if you led anyone in the sinner's prayer. You don't have to pray for the sick. You don't have to cast out any demons. All that is required is that you talk to these people and get to know them." But they're still unsure.

You should stand back and watch what happens when we actually get out on the streets. One timid young believer begins to talk with one of the street people. He finds that person is sick and hurting. You hear him begin praying for the sick.

Another talks to a man who has never heard of Jesus and who doesn't know why his life is so confused. You'll begin hearing the gospel presented.

Still another from my group talks with a previous member of a satanic cult. Soon you will hear a demon being cast out by the authority of Jesus' name through the lips of a novice disciple who didn't know he was capable of doing such things. He has discovered something about the life he possesses that was previously only a theory.

Life is a discovery! Every command of God is intended to release us from the bondage of who we aren't into the wonderful world of who we were meant to be. And every circumstance is an opportunity to find another nugget of the divine life which has been deposited into our bosoms.

Our experience here on the planet earth was never meant to be one of mere survival. We are ambassadors of heaven. We represent a new realm which operates under a government vastly different from the one operating in this physical world.

When we relegate our life to a "rat race" or getting our "piece of the pie," we've missed it. It is so much more than that. In fact, the apostle Paul says it like this:

> ... Just as it is written, "Things which eye has not seen and ear has not heard, and which have not entered the heart of man, all that God has prepared for those who love Him." For to us God revealed them through the Spirit; for the Spirit searches all things, even the depths of God. **1 Cor 2:9-10**

IT'S YOUR CHOICE

Now, don't miss the important distinction in all this advice to "become what you were meant to be." It's not something you can do on your own! It only happens as we live in relationship with the Father.

And the choice is ours. There are still two trees in the garden. Even though we are programmed by our "new birth" nature for obedience to God, we have also been programmed by generations of disobedience to follow in Adam's footsteps. So my choice is: Do I act according to my nature as defined by God, or do I act according to my other programming and continue gathering the fruit of the "be to do" tree?

But how do we make our choice? It's hard to escape "do to be" fever. And remember what I said earlier: Once that fruit is eaten, human beings never get over the need to perform until we die.

That might sound like a hopeless situation, but there is, in fact, good news. There is a way out. You can die.

"Some good news," you grumble. Wait. It *is* good news, because another Adam went into the garden and ate of the tree of life. He didn't have to die, but he did so on behalf of all those infected by the "do to be" fruit. And he made it possible for us to die with him. He not only paid the penalty for our rebellion, but he took us with him in his death, burial, and resurrection so that we can live a new kind of life.

We are no longer merely children of the first Adam. By faith, we can be children of Jesus, the last Adam. This choice —simply to believe or not—is our privilege. We choose the tree of life by believing in him.

But that puts us in a vulnerable position. Choosing a life of relationship with God means giving up our independence. It means becoming dependent on someone other than ourselves—Jesus—for the resources of life. When we become that dependent on someone, he had better be trustworthy.

If Jesus didn't fully pay our debt, we are eternally damned. If he failed to please the Father, we are displeasing to the Father also. If his shed blood did not satisfy the guilt of our trespasses, we stand forever guilty before the throne of God. If he is not resurrected from the dead, we are hopeless.

But... if he did these things, then we can be free from the shackles of "do to be." We can live our lives in a relationship with God the Father just as Jesus did while he was on earth. He is our life. He is our wisdom. He is our righteousness. He is our sanctification. He is our resource for everything we will ever need to do or have.

So, what are my options?

I can continue to eke out an existence on earth characterized by the performing fruit of the "do to be" tree.

Or I can die... by faith in the one who died for me and gave me a whole new dimension of life. When I do that, I make the choice to be what God intended me to be all along. I choose to live with him in the realm where all performance is complete and where I can depend wholly on him.

PART TWO

Grace and the Pharisee in Me

"For I say to you, that unless your righteousness surpasses that of the scribes and Pharisees, you shall not enter the kingdom of heaven." **Matthew 5:20**

CHAPTER

3 Blinded by Religion

WHEN GOD'S LIFE took on flesh in his Son Jesus, the most obvious and constant opposition came from the counterfeit life offered by the religious-oriented Jewish leaders. Most of the ordinary people simply ignored Jesus (or followed him). But the Pharisees and many other religious people felt he was a threat. They not only opposed him openly; their opposition was accompanied by an aggressive anger that sought to destroy him.

That phenomenon is still around today. And many in the "pagan pool" of the multitudes will respond positively to the Christ-like qualities real Christians display. Others will see the Christian life as foolishness and simply respond in apathy. A few may actually mock Christians as "simpleminded." But the real opposition will again come from the counterfeit version of life—human religion. Since all human religion grows from the "do to be" tree, it always has as its basis conforming our behavior to certain criteria.

This is legalism. It was personified in the Pharisees of Jesus' day. But don't make the mistake of seeing the Pharisees as the comical characters depicted by church-bulletin cartoons. They were well-respected men of their day—not only theologians, but also revered leaders to whom the people looked for spiritual guidance. We have assigned to them such a ridiculous reputation that it is hard for some of us to identify with some of their characteristics. But the truth is, they were not all that different from some of us today. The Pharisees are all around us. The Pharisees, in fact, may live inside you and me.

THE MARK OF A PHARISEE

What is the mark of a Pharisee—modern or ancient? One of the telltale characteristics is *spiritual blindness.* Pharisees are people who are so focused on their religion that they cannot see the spiritual reality in front of their noses.

At the beginning of Jesus' ministry, he went to his hometown and attended the synagogue on the Sabbath. While he was there, he was asked to read the Scriptures. Taking the scroll, he read from Isaiah 61 the passage that referred to his own mission statement: "The Spirit of the Lord is upon me, because he has anointed me to preach the gospel to the poor. He has sent me to proclaim release to the captives, and recovery of sight to the blind, to set free those who are downtrodden, to proclaim the favorable year of the Lord." Then, when he had finished reading, he did a remarkable thing. He handed the scroll back to the attendant and said, "Today this Scripture has been fulfilled in your hearing" (Lk 4:18-19, 21).

What an astounding statement! What an astounding scene! Here we have the living Word reading the written Word and explaining it to his listeners. (This is a picture of the way the New Testament believer is to regard the Bible—not as God's regulation manual, but as a book to be interpreted by the living Word who lives within us in the person of the Holy Spirit.)

But even on this occasion the religious leaders could not see what was going on. What blindness! Not only did they refuse to receive Jesus' declaration of who he was; they were so enraged by that declaration they set about to kill him.

This revelation of religious blindness was to be the atmosphere in which Jesus, the Light of the World, was to operate. The Pharisees never saw the kingdom Jesus talked about. Their eyes were truly closed to the reality of what he was about; they saw only the external appearance. As a result, they heard him talk of "eating my flesh and drinking my blood" and thought he was crazy. They heard him say, "Destroy this temple and in three days I will rebuild it" and tried to kill him because they thought he was a threat to the physical temple in Jerusalem.

A TALE OF BLINDNESS… AND HEALING

One of the most amusing stories in all the Bible is the story of the blind people in John 9. Blindness is obviously the subject of this chapter, but the man who is physically blind is only a minor player.

Here is the scene as I have paraphrased it: Jesus and his disciples are walking along and spot a man who has been blind from birth. The disciples begin questioning their teacher as to why the blind man is afflicted in this manner. Jesus cut through the matrix of their theological confusion and basically says that the man is blind so the glory of God can be revealed in him.

Then Jesus does something that seems very strange to the rational minds gathered around him. He takes a mixture of saliva and dirt, packs the mud on the blind man's eyes, and tells him to go across town to wash the dirt from his eyes.

Now admittedly, this is not a common practice among ophthalmologists. I'm sure those in town had many questions about Jesus' method of healing.

"How does dirt in one's eye promote healing?"

"Isn't it bad enough to be blind? Do you also have to have spit and dirt in your face?"

"Has healing ever been done this way before?"

However, when the blind man in obedience goes across town and washes the dirt from his eyes, he discovers to his amazement that the darkness has also gone! He rushes back to his neighborhood, thrilled that he can see.

But here's where the humor begins. In the face of this incredible miracle, all the man's former associates begin acting very strangely. It's as if they just can't handle the fact that something wonderful has broken into their lives.

The former blind man's neighbors, for instance, start quibbling about whether this is even the same person. After all, the guy they knew was blind... this man can see. Apparently, it is easier to doubt the healed man's identity than to believe in the miraculous power of this man Jesus.

Even the man's *parents* react with cautious enthusiasm. They seem to fear the consequences of knowingly accepting their son's account of a miraculous healing brought about in such an unconventional way. So they take the man to the Pharisees. I suppose they want the opinion of those who are qualified to make judgments in these matters. So they call on the religious leaders of their day. And the Pharisees begin asking their questions.

Can you see how ridiculous it all is? Neither neighbors nor parents nor Pharisees have thus far congratulated the man on being able to see. Nobody can rejoice over his liberation because they can't understand how it happened!

In the course of their questioning, the Pharisees discover that the man has been healed on the Sabbath. They're absolutely sure that this could not be a work of God, for God would not desecrate the Sabbath by healing a man of blindness. However, they're in a quandary: "How does a sinner, such as this man Jesus, do miracles like opening blind eyes?"

The Pharisees decide to call the man's parents and question them more thoroughly. And the parents are so afraid of being thrown out of the synagogue that even though they know exactly who healed their son and how it happened, they hedge in front of the Pharisees. How silly they look at this point! Their desire to be accepted by the religious community is so great that they are willing to deny the gracious Lord who had given sight to their poor blind son.

It's obviously a matter of the blind man seeing and the seeing people choosing to be blind. The Pharisees continue questioning the man and he keeps repeating the same story until he finally asks, with a hint of sarcasm, "Why do you keep asking me? Do you want to be his disciples, too?" And in their angered response to this question, the Pharisees reveal their primary problem: "You're his disciple, but we're disciples of Moses."

BELIEVING IS SEEING

These religious people had made the conscious decision to receive the revelation of God that came through Moses but to never go beyond that point. Because of this, a veil hung over their spiritual faces so they could see nothing that had not been revealed through Moses.

Paul made this point very clearly in 2 Corinthians 3:12-16:

> Having therefore such a hope, we use great boldness in our speech, and are not as Moses, who used to put a veil over his face that the sons of Israel might not look intently at the end of what was fading away. But their minds were hardened; for until this very day at the reading of the old covenant the same veil remains unlifted, because it is removed in Christ. But to this day whenever Moses is read, a veil lies over their heart; but whenever a man turns to the Lord, the veil is taken away.

He was clearly referring to the Old Testament story of Moses' coming down from Mount Sinai after receiving the Ten Commandments. When he came down from the mountain, his face shone with the glory of God. This evidently brought fear to the people, so Moses put a veil over his face.

The people so looked to Moses as their intermediary with God that he became their interpretive tool. It was as if the people made a decision, "Moses, you hear God and tell us what he says. We don't want to hear him for ourselves. That glory stuff is too scary." (See Exodus 19:12 and Hebrews 12:18-19.)

That, obviously, was the tack the Pharisees were taking.

Rather than risk a confrontation with God, they chose to stay behind a veil, relying on intermediaries such as Moses to interpret God for them. They were choosing their blindness.

And many of us today choose our blindness as well. We've elected to put up a veil that limits our understanding of what God says. We've relied on a denomination or a particular preacher or a particular doctrine to define for us the reality of God. We have reduced him to a system of theology and have tried to capture him in the limited understanding of the human mind.

But God will not be captured like that. He refuses to be contained in our theological boxes. He refuses to fit our denominational definitions. Most important, he will not lower himself to simply giving answers to our rational minds while leaving us in the quagmire of our problems. It seems as though our gracious God's intent is to heal us rather than answer all our questions—to give us sight rather than explain why we became blind.

And how do we begin to receive that gift of sight?

The psalmist said, "I would have despaired *unless I had believed that I would see* the goodness of the Lord in the land of the living" (Ps 27:13, emphasis mine). The Pharisees, however, refused to believe, so they were never able to see.

May I remind you, if you are tempted at this point to come down hard on the Pharisees, that it is very difficult for any of us to lay aside our previous perceptions of who God is and how he works and take on broader revelation. Doing that means—at least for a time—becoming vulnerable and insecure. We have to lay our time-honored concepts on the altar to be examined by God himself. If they are valid, he will return them to us. If they are not, he will take them away and free us from their deluding influences.

Jesus really did come to give sight to the blind, and he was not just talking about the physically blind. Spiritual eyesight is a gift that comes through the grace of God. It is your inheritance as a faith-person. Believe it and see!

CHAPTER 4

Mercy or Sacrifice

WITHOUT QUESTION, Jesus lived the purest, simplest, and most satisfying life of anyone who has ever been on the planet earth. So why was he so persecuted by the religionists of his day? What did the Pharisees have against him?

Or, to hit closer to home, why do so many people—Christians included—live such restricted, loveless lives? Why are people who preach about God's love so afraid to abandon themselves to it? Why are "good" people so angry, so defensive, so abusive of one another? Why do they insist on being blind?

It could be that the answer to all those questions is the same: the legalistic mindset. And maybe we can get some clues about how that way of thinking works by examining the struggle between Jesus and his "religious" adversaries.

THE CRUCIAL DISTINCTION

According to Jesus, the Pharisees kept their feet in their mouths because *they did not know the difference between mercy and sacrifice.* That difference defines for us the vast chasm that separates life from legalism.

Now, the concept of sacrifice looms large in all the world's religions—from the radical ritual of burning children on an altar to satisfy some distorted deity to the subtle act of believing that something I do will get God to move on my behalf. The idea of sacrifice is rooted in the hearts of religious people everywhere. (And all of us are religious, whether we realize it or not. We have all been looking for a way back to God since Adam and Eve fell and were cast out of the Garden of Eden.)

And there's a reason the notion of sacrifice is so widespread. God started it. All through history, and all over the world, people have responded to a God-given instinct that sacrifice is necessary to deal with the problem of human sin and estrangement.

The word *sacrifice* literally refers to the act of giving up something we own—something important to us—for something more important, especially to find favor with God. It also may involve giving up something—especially, offering something living—as a way of paying for one's sins or gaining favor with God. In Jesus' day, Jewish religious practice involved the sacrifice of animals as a "blood offering" for one's sins.

In the truest sense, then, only God can sacrifice, for he is the owner of everything. But in making us stewards of his possessions, he also taught us the concept of relinquishing something valuable as a route to restoring relationships and making wrong things right again.

There is something overwhelmingly beautiful in this concept as it is expressed through Jesus, who willingly offered his life as the Lamb of God. It was to that supreme Sacrifice—the supreme act of grace and mercy—that Old Testament sacrifices pointed. And it is by faith in him that we are given the privilege of making sacrifices in our own lives—giving up what may be important to us in the interest of gaining a greater good—through the power of his life in us.

But the Pharisees' problem—shared by millions of Jesus' day, before, and after—was that they mistakenly believed that their sacrifices actually *paid for* their blessings. The Pharisees honestly believed they could do something or give something that would cause God to act benevolently toward them.

The Pharisees were operating according to an "I act and God responds" mentality. Because they made the right sacrifices, they declared *themselves* to be right. And in so doing, they totally missed the point of the act of sacrifice.

God had instituted the sacrificial system in the first place not to teach that sacrifice was God's greatest pleasure, but to demonstrate that sin was a serious violation of God's character and could only be atoned for by the shedding of innocent blood. But that very teaching was given to the Jewish people as an act of *mercy*—a way for God's people to receive cleansing for their sins.

The Pharisees were experts in the interpretation of biblical law. And yet, because of their legalistic perspective, they had missed the essence of this Old Testament teaching and had only embraced the shell. They never understood that God acted first in mercy so that we could respond in faith—that sacrifice is meaningless unless it is a response to God's love. And as a result of their misunderstandings, they became trapped by their own legalism.

WHAT GOD DESIRES

Twice in the New Testament, Jesus nailed the Pharisees concerning their legalistic ignorance about the meaning of sacrifice.

First, in Matthew 9, we find Jesus eating with Matthew and some of his tax collector buddies. These were not the most respectable people of their day; in fact, they were the equivalent of today's Mafia. Yet Jesus and a few of his disciples were having dinner with these undesirables. The religious Pharisees, seeing this, believed they had found a great occasion to accuse Jesus. It was unthinkable to the religious mind that holy people would associate with unholy people.

Jesus' answer to their accusation revealed the essence of God's attitude toward life: "It is not those who are healthy who need a physician, but those who are sick" (Mt 9:12). And then Jesus quoted the prophet Hosea to them, giving some good advice which, by the way, they never heeded. "Go and learn what this means, 'I desire compassion, and not sacrifice.'"

Jesus quoted that same verse from Hosea on another occasion as well. He and his disciples had been walking through the grain field on the Sabbath. Becoming hungry, they plucked some grain from the standing stalks. The moment they did, the Pharisees jumped up from their hiding places and accused them of breaking the Sabbath. Jesus once again responded to the situation by saying, "But if you had known what this means, 'I desire compassion and not a sacrifice,' you would not have condemned the innocent" (Mt 12:7).

In each of these situations, Jesus was pinpointing a particular pitfall of the legalistic mindset—a specific danger of misunderstanding sacrifice. What are these pitfalls?

PITFALL #1: AVOIDING SINNERS

First of all, the Pharisees' misunderstanding of sacrifice had caused them to develop a fearful and dangerous *doctrine of avoidance.*

God had given his people a set of laws to help them be a "light to the nations." But the religious leaders of Jesus' day had taken those very laws and developed a philosophy that assumed, "Darkness always defeats light, dirt always defiles clean, death is stronger than life, and sin ruins righteousness." They were experts in the washing of their hands and the cleansing of their cups, but had no concept of how hearts could be cleansed. As a result, their only possible response to a sinful world was to steer clear of it. No wonder they were so offended that Jesus ate with tax collectors and sinners!

Today's Pharisees live with the same "avoidance mentality."

Rather than focusing on the liberty to rule and reign through Jesus Christ, they obsess about the avoidance of evil. "We can't afford to be around evil people; their evil might rub off on us" seems to be the prevailing mentality. As a result, much of the church has retreated inside its walls and put up stained glass so they can't see outside. They have settled for being an inbred community that plays religious games of sacrifice while the wicked world is left to rot and decay in darkness.

This obviously is not the life Jesus came to bring. He came to set men and women free from the fear of darkness and rottenness. He showed us how to rule and reign in every circumstance through faith in a sovereign and merciful God.

At the very inauguration of his ministry, in fact, Jesus made some very remarkable statements—statements that were radical to the ears of the religious. "You are the light of the world... the salt of the earth." Jesus was saying that mere humans can be of such godly essence that wherever they go darkness has to flee, that in their presence putrefaction is defeated.

Because of this, there's no reason for God's people to fear darkness, dirt, death, or sin. After all, there's never been an occasion in all the history of the universe where light has backed away from the presence of darkness. There is no darkness so intimidating that it can defeat the smallest ray of light. Light is always the victor, never the victim.

Jesus commissioned his disciples to go into all the world, being the light and salt. He told them to occupy until the King returned for his own. And that's the message we must remember when the legalistic mindset threatens to cut us off from the world outside.

It's an unequivocal fact that a fearful church will never positively effect the world. But we need not fear the power of sin and perversion. We can be the aggressors rather than the victims. Our life is stronger than their death. Our hope is higher than their dreams. And our message is good news to the needy, not "good luck, buddy."

But, a word of caution here. Some trying to overcome this

"scared legalism" have been victims of guilty love. That is, they feel that in order to prove they are the light of the world and the salt of the earth, they must go into the worst places and retrieve the poor sinners.

There may indeed be times when we have to reach past our comfort zone or even face danger in order to go where God is leading us—but we don't have to do these things to prove anything. We don't have to handle snakes to prove that we believe. We don't have to redeem pimps to prove that we love. Life means being free to go where God directs without fear and without guilt.

This is important to understand because guilty love is really just another form of legalism. When we act out of guilty love, we are operating out of the same "avoidance of evil" mentality that waylaid the Pharisees—only this time we are fearfully avoiding the evil of unconcern or lack of compassion. Legalistic love can destroy life just as quickly as legalistic isolationism.

A few years ago I was a part of a group of men that went to Colorado for a retreat. The retreat setting was absolutely beautiful. The camp was nestled in the heart of the mountains, and the main cabin backed up to a sheer cliff of about two thousand feet.

One of the rules of the camp was that no one was to try climbing that mountain. But some of the men in our group obviously took that prohibition as a challenge. The next afternoon they attempted to climb the cliff. One of the men made it to within thirty feet of the top. At that point he became entrapped in a crevice, unable either to ascend or descend without falling off the mountain. His companions, seeing his plight, returned to camp for help. By this time there was only a half hour of daylight left. The man on the mountain was in great danger—not only of falling off the mountain but, since he was wearing only shorts and a T-shirt, of hypothermia.

Now, I was one of the men in charge of this retreat. It had been my suggestion that we come to this particular camp, and I had been a leader in getting the men there and ministering to them. I bore much of the responsibility for what went on. So as I stood at the bottom of that sheer cliff, straining my eyes to find the wayward victim, I had to deal with some pretty sharp thoughts: "Should I climb up there and get him?... Do I love him enough to do that?... Will these men think I don't love him if I don't go get him?... Will I be perceived as being irresponsible if I don't go get him?"

I can honestly say I did not spend much time arguing with myself over these thoughts. Instead, I made some vital decisions. Yes, I did love him enough to go get him. But I loved him *more* than that. Knowing that I was not an expert mountain climber and that I would put both our lives in jeopardy if I attempted to rescue him, I determined that I loved him enough to call for someone who could really help. So I hurriedly called a rescue squad from a neighboring town. I watched as true experts climbed the mountain in the darkness and brought him back down that sheer cliff safely in their arms.

A perverted "guilty love" will force us into situations where we try to prove our love. Real love, however, liberates us to think clearly, follow Jesus' leading, and then actually do what is best for everyone concerned. And only that kind of love will free you from the pitfalls of legalistic thinking.

PITFALL #2: INSTITUTIONS OVER INDIVIDUALS

Another dead giveaway to the presence of a legalistic mindset is that it inevitably elevates the value of institutions above the value of individuals. It was this kind of shallow thinking that made the Pharisees ready to stone Jesus and his disciples for "desecrating" the Sabbath. But Jesus quickly pointed out that these "experts" in biblical interpretation had missed some important points in the very Old Testament that they were using as their guide.

At one time, for instance, David and his men had been

given the show bread from the temple, a bread that was never to be used by anybody except the priests. Jesus also pointed out the seemingly obvious reality in that the priests of his day broke the Sabbath every week by working. Because of their insistence on keeping their understanding of the law, they were not only undervaluing individuals whom God loved, but also missing the true meaning of Scripture.

One of the chief characteristics of the legalistic mindset is that it shuts one's eyes to the panorama and beauty of God's eternal truth and reduces that truth to a set of rules, regulations, and restrictions. Then God's words become stones to break people rather than life to enable people. When this legalistic mindset is adopted to any degree in any society, the church becomes an instrument of pain rather than an instrument of healing. I've seen it happen again and again.

Innumerable people have been rejected or ignored because they did not hold to some particular interpretation of nonessential doctrines. I have known many a pastor who was asked to resign "for the good of the church" when the church leaders were simply unwilling to shoulder the responsibility of managing relationships. It is easier to "get a new one" than to forbear one another and accept our differences. This religious mentality is as foolish as it is harsh.

Here's another example. I want to be one found eternally standing on the pro side of family. I would never be found supporting anything that takes away from or diminishes holy matrimony or family. And yet I have watched in horror as religion, in an effort to keep the institution of marriage holy, makes the single and the divorced feel like second-class citizens. Divorce is at best an unpleasant reality for everyone involved, including husband, wife, children, family, and friends. It inevitably causes wounds that turn into scars. If it can be avoided, it should be avoided.

But the fact is, divorce does happen. And I am convinced that desecrating and devaluing those who have experienced divorce does not add to the sanctity of marriage!

Several years ago I was involved in a counseling situation with a couple who were having trouble in their marriage. We had met on several occasions, and I thought they were making progress in salvaging their relationship, only to be informed on about our sixth session that they were giving up; they had mutually agreed that divorce was their only solution.

As I drove away from my office that day, I was expressing my anger and frustration in the form of a prayer. If you had been there you would have defined it as "Dudley fussing with God."

"Why are they giving up?" I fumed. "Don't they know what this is doing to them, to their children? Don't they know they are creating hurts in their psyche that may take years to heal? Do they not realize they are saying to their children that commitment means nothing, that one's word has no value? Do they not know that they are even hurting the cause of the gospel because they are diluting and redefining the concept of covenant and commitment? Why God, I went on, "they're even hurting your reputation."

Then, as clearly as I have ever heard, my heavenly Father talked to me in my spirit. As I listened, his thoughts surfaced: "If you're worried about my reputation, I've taken care of it. My integrity can never be impugned. When my holiness was violated, my own Son paid the ultimate price by his death on the cross. No one will never be able to say that I am unholy. So the reputation that I want to convey is that I care for broken people."

I am absolutely not saying that any subjective impression I have takes precedence over the revelation of Scripture. But that experience in prayer caused me to see a broader perspective of Scripture than I had ever seen before. I do not want ever to be accused of condemning persons in an effort to uphold an institution.

There are so many bruised warriors out there—victims of a legalistic mindset. There is Mr. Martin, a seventy-four-year-old saint who was disqualified as a prospective candidate for deacon because he had two sons who smoked. The reason for the disqualification of Mr. Martin was as follows. "The Scriptures teach that a man must rule his house well if he is to be a leader. Since these two boys smoke, Mr. Martin, their father, is disqualified." But these "two boys" were aged fifty and fifty-four!

I read in the newspaper one day that some fundamentalist Christians were fighting the establishment of a winery in a particular town. One of the leaders was opposing it on the biblical grounds that drinking wine was a sin. He was asked by the reporter, "Didn't Jesus turn water into wine?" The response was, "I suppose so, but I don't know why he did. That has always been an embarrassment to me."

That attitude is not an uncommon reality when our concept of life is limited to a set of "do's and don'ts" that define what is right. Jesus will often prove to be an embarrassment to the religious mind.

Jesus made it very clear, "Man was not made for the Sabbath, but the Sabbath for man."

It is too easy to justify our harsh treatment of individuals with the rationalization that the effectiveness of the church or any other organization must be protected. When the individual proves to be imperfect and have weaknesses, we tend to sacrifice him or her to keep the productivity of the organization going. But this kind of injustice is not a part of the life of God.

Life, as Jesus defined it, is relationship. That relationship is not and cannot be bound by rules and regulations. Our legalistic tendency is to reduce God to a set of concepts and confine him to a theological and philosophical system where certain interpretations become all that we see. When that happens, we easily neglect the whole of God's revelation.

PITFALL #3: REDUCING A RELATIONSHIP TO A FORMULA

So we can see from the two confrontations between Jesus and the Pharisees that a perverted sense of sacrifice produces two destructive views of life. First, fearing the power of evil tends to lead to a doctrine of avoidance in which righteousness is determined by evils that are avoided rather than by good that is expressed. Second, the focus on proper external behavior typically results in condemning the individual while protecting the institution. But perhaps the most dangerous pitfall of the legalistic mindset is that it *reduces a tender relationship with God to a formula.*

It is interesting that legalists often make the accusation that stressing grace leads to license. But it is the legalist who presumes on the grace of God with an emphasis on right actions, right rituals, and right restrictions.

This is made very clear in the original Old Testament passage that Jesus quoted to the Pharisees. Hosea's statement that God desires mercy, not sacrifice, was spoken to a people who had broken their covenant with God and then tried to "bribe" him with sacrifices. God's people had been disobedient by not responding to him in love and faith, so he had allowed the discipline of hard times to come upon them. Things were so tough that they decided they needed to do something to gain relief. They had seen God's acts in the past and concluded, "If we will say all the right words, God will relent of all this pressure he is putting on us and restore us to our original condition."

Hosea used the image of romantic love to dramatize Israel's faithlessness. He pictured God as the husband and Israel as a bride who had not only committed adultery but become a harlot. As a nation, it had sold itself to other gods for protection, provision, and guidance. And then, when God's people were reaping the whirlwind of the wind they had sown, their solution was "Let's do the right thing to get God to respond to us."

See how they are undervaluing the relationship? Do you see the revealed legalistic mentality that "what I do determines what God does"? God is reduced to a button to be pushed so that relief can come our way. His whole kingdom is reduced to principles that can be applied so we can experience life without hassle. This is, in essence, religious idolatry. It is a human being saying, "I am in charge, and I have discovered how to use God for my own benefit."

This kind of mentality takes the wonderful promises of God and reduces them to formulas. For instance, one of the most popular Scriptures used among Bible-believing Christians is 2 Chronicles 7:14: "[If] my people who are called by my name humble themselves and pray, and seek my face and turn from their wicked ways, then I will hear from heaven, will forgive their sin, and will heal their land."

This is a wonderful promise of God. It is God stating to his people "Come back into proper relationship with me. We can have life together at its fullest." But instead of hearing this promise, so many Christians have reduced it to a formula that, when applied, will guarantee that relief will come.

I've personally dealt with numbers of people who were trying their best to "get right with God." Usually they were confused and disillusioned as a result of their efforts. They were absolutely convinced that they were full of sin and did not know how to get free. But then I would share the wonderful promise of God from 1 John 1:9: "If we confess our sins, he is faithful and just to forgive us our sins, and to cleanse us from all unrighteousness." And they would reply, "I've already tried that, and it didn't work."

What they were really saying was, "I used the formula, but there was no relief." The problem is, a relationship is not a formula. The gift of grace is not a combination of requirements that gets results, but an invitation for full fellowship. The solution to sin is mercy, not sacrifice; life, not legalism; relationship, not religion.

The "I can get God to act" mentality has reduced all of the wonderful disciplines of the Christian life into hard work. If I pray long enough and hard enough, surely I can get God to act on my behalf. If I fast long enough and sincerely enough, I will get relief. If I go to church, maybe God will be appeased. Etcetera. Ad nauseam.

God is not a big computer in the sky waiting for us to enter the proper code word. He has already acted on our behalf and made his life and mercy available to us. His promises to us are not trick formulas that enable us to manage and manipulate our lives here on earth. They're invitations to a fresh encounter and an everlasting relationship with him.

Those who live by the sacrifice mentality are never quite sure they've sacrificed enough. Those who live by mercy realize that all it takes to receive mercy is to have a need and be honest about it. Those who approach God on the basis of their sacrifice receive only disappointment. Those who approach him on the basis of mercy receive all that he has, because faith in mercy is heaven's currency.

UNCONTRIVED JOY

Mercy receivers know that it wasn't their initiative toward God that established their relationship with him. Instead, they were wooed by his love and simply responded by faith. When we couldn't go to him, he came to us.

What's the result of that gut-deep knowledge? Joy. Mercy receivers can live with eternal joy in their spirit.

Watching religious people trying to be joyful is amusing. For many, joy is a contrived behavior. After all, joy is a mark of being "right with God"—to the legalistic mind, an absolute requirement. And so they often try to put on a joyful face lest their lives somehow become suspect.

Periodically I find myself watching a beauty pageant with my teenage daughter. Watching beauty pageants is not so much fun, but being with my daughter is. She is really good at picking the winner; usually she will have picked the top five the first few minutes of the pageant. I always enjoy seeing whether or not she is right.

But there is one part of the proceedings I have always disliked. It's the time when the emcee, creating great anticipation with his body language, begins to open the envelope: "...

And the second runner-up is..." I get butterflies in my stomach, because I know that some girl is about to be put into a terrible situation.

Think of it. Second runner-up. You didn't win, but you didn't lose. She is trying to smile and receive the congratulations from the others amiably, but you know she is disappointed. Her attitude has to be, "Wow, I wish I were number one, but thank God I'm not number fifty." She is not a loser, because she was in the top three. But she is not a winner, either. Her smile is contrived. She's like hundreds of Christians who are trying to be joyful when, in fact, they are aware they were not good enough to be number one.

Notice the difference when the winner is revealed? There is no contrived happiness there. She begins to cry and laugh and hug and dance... and she always knocks her crown off. She exudes spontaneous joy, because she is aware that she has attained the highest place in this pageant.

That's the mentality of those who relate to God on the basis of mercy. His mercy gives us all that Jesus paid for or we get nothing. We are either accepted totally, forgiven absolutely by the shedding of his blood and loved unconditionally in his heart, or we get nothing. He does not dole it out in little bits as we make payments to him. It is only those who live by their sacrifice who have that mentality.

But the legalistic mindset doesn't have to be yours. You don't have to contrive your joy. Why? Because you won the pageant! Because Jesus has been raised by God to sit at the right hand of the Father forever, and you have been placed in him. You receive what Jesus deserves because he took on himself what you deserve. Because you know his forgiveness, you don't have to work to pay for your sins through acts of sacrifice. Because you know his acceptance, you are free from performing for merit. You can live joyful in the knowledge that you are a recipient of his mercy and therefore a channel of mercy to others who, like yourself, can never qualify for anything *other* than mercy!

CHAPTER 5

Spirit and Flesh

WHAT IS THE PRIMARY problem with Pharisees of all ages—both in Jesus' day and today? What makes them so hard to live with... and so miserable inside?

As we have seen, part of the problem is that Pharisees choose to look only through a veil—to limit their understanding to preconceived notions. Because they fail to understand that God wants mercy instead of sacrifice—relationship, not religion—they spend a lot of their energy avoiding evil and upholding institutions. But Pharisees also run into problems because they set their minds on the *flesh* instead of the *spirit*.

Sound surprising? After all, Pharisees may be judgmental and legalistic, but most of them pride themselves in their avoidance of "fleshly sins." They make a point not to indulge in the kind of vices that Galatians 5 listed as "deeds of the flesh"—"immorality, impurity, sensuality, idolatry, sorcery... jealousy, outbursts of anger," and so on.

But as a quick look at Pharisees then and now will show, religionized flesh can be just as rotten as secularized flesh.

DEATH VERSUS LIFE AND PEACE

But just what harm does living in the flesh do? What are the consequences of fleshly thinking, whether secular or religious? The apostle Paul spelled it out starkly in his Letter to the Romans: "The mind set on the flesh is death" (Rom 8:6).

On the most basic level, of course, those who live in the flesh will not inherit eternal life. But death, according to the context of this passage, would also include:

- no energy from the Spirit, thus fatigue,
- no vision from the Spirit, thus frustration,
- no ability to please God, thus failure.

Unbelievers are limited in their choices. They live in the flesh and can have no other real focus. Because they live separated from real life, they have no eternal energy, vision, or ability. They are restricted to natural life (1 Cor 2:14) with its built-in limitations.

Believers, however, do have a choice. They can see the realm of the Spirit. They have a perception of eternal life that affects them now as well as then. But if believers choose not to set their minds "on the things above" (Col 3:2), they will experience the deadening effect of the flesh in their daily life. They are choosing death where they could have life.

When there is no life emanating from the Spirit, we operate in our own strength. No wonder we quickly grow exhausted. We attempt to follow our own vision and are therefore frustrated as to our mission, objectives, and goals. And we have no ability to please God because the mind set on the flesh is hostile toward God. The result is a constant sense of failure, no matter how fine our religious performance may be.

But there's a positive alternative to that kind of living death. Paul sets that down clearly as well in the continuation of this passage: "The mind set on the Spirit is life and peace."

Paul means not only that those who live in the Spirit will be prepared for eternal life, but also that those who focus on the Spirit will exude life and peace at all times, in their daily lives. They're the kind of people who encourage you when you're around them, energize you as you talk to them, and influence you in your decisions because of the obvious spiritual ambiance in their lives. They may not be the most intelligent people you've ever known, nor do they have all the answers to life's complex problems. They are certainly not immune from sorrow and difficulty (not even Jesus could claim such an immunity), but still the very life of God shines through these people. They're fun to be with, for they never seem to be controlled by their circumstances. Their perspective of life is simple and peaceful. Although they may face tragic situations, they choose to stand firm on a solid rock.

WHAT DOES "FLESH" LOOK LIKE?

When you consider these consequences—"death" as opposed to "life and peace," the fleshly mindset begins to lose its appeal. But how do we recognize "fleshly thinking" in the first place? As I have indicated, fleshly thinking isn't always manifested by "bad" behavior.

In fact, if we consider only obviously negative behavior, we may miss the essence of this "spirit versus flesh" truth. For the flesh is something far more subtle than bad deeds—and that's why religious people can be just as "flesh-focused" as brawlers, pimps, and winos.

Maybe the greatest passage describing the flesh is Philippians 3:3-7:

> For we... worship in the Spirit of God and glory in Christ Jesus and put no confidence in the flesh.... If anyone else has a mind to put confidence in the flesh, I far more: circumcised the eighth day, of the nation of Israel, of the tribe of Benjamin, a Hebrew of Hebrews; as to the Law, a Pharisee; as to zeal, a persecutor of the church; as to the righteousness which is in the Law, found blameless. But whatever things were gain to me, those things I have counted as loss for the sake of Christ.

Four aspects of fleshly thinking are listed in this passage, each one (after the first) indicated by the phrase "as to":

- *the natural* ("circumcised on the eighth day, of the nation of Israel, of the tribe of Benjamin, a Hebrew of Hebrews")
- *outward conformity* ("*as to* the Law, a Pharisee")
- *human zeal* ("*as to* zeal, a persecutor of the church")
- *self-righteousness* ("*as to* the righteousness which is in the Law, found blameless")

Let's examine these four characteristics of the flesh in a little more detail:

Aspect #1—The Natural As Opposed to the Spiritual. Paul speaks of belonging to the nation of Israel and the tribe of Benjamin, having been circumcised on the eighth day according to Jewish custom—of being a "Hebrew of the Hebrews." All of this refers to his natural, physical relationships, as opposed to the supernatural, spiritual relationship. That would be like my saying, "Well, I am one of an old family here in town—my father was the mayor and my mother served on the town council. And we trace our family line directly back to Henry VIII of England." Or, in a more religious setting, I might boast, "I come from a long line of preachers; my grandparents began the missions program in my denomination, and my father has been both a preacher and a teacher for forty years."

The point is, I would be focusing on my natural connections in the human community. And Paul makes it clear that those who live in the Spirit "put no confidence" in such things.

Aspect #2—Outward Conformity As Opposed to Inward Transformation. When Paul says, "as to the Law, a Pharisee," he was speaking of a group with which he had chosen to affiliate himself. He was a Pharisee, one who held strictly to the rules of his religious community. It would be something like saying, "I attended such-and-such a church for forty years without missing a Sunday. I was a deacon and a committee chairman, and I always tithed. I also refrained from drinking or smoking because that would have looked bad for someone in my position."

And, once again surprisingly, Paul says that those who live in the Spirit don't really worry about that kind of belonging.

Aspect #3—Human Zeal As Opposed to Divine Passion. Paul's particular zeal as a Pharisee had been to persecute the church. A modern Pharisee might throw similar enthusiasm into causes and crusades—from banning abortion to saving the environment, from eliminating sexist language in hymnals to eliminating those who advocate changing the hymnals!

And regardless of the particular content of the crusades, Paul would vote "no confidence" to them *if* carried on out of ordinary human passion.

Aspect #4—Self-Righteousness As Opposed to Faith Righteousness. Paul pointed out that in his Pharisee days he had been absolutely blameless according to the Law. He had kept all the rules diligently. He had the same kind of confidence in his own righteousness as a modern Pharisee who boasts, "I have never stolen nor murdered nor committed adultery—I have never even taken the Lord's name in vain!" And once again, Paul indicates that keeping all the rules does not protect one from fleshly thinking.

WHY "GOOD" DOESN'T CUT IT

Now, notice that none of these four aspects of living "in the flesh" sounds all that bad. Isn't it good to be proud of your family and align yourself with worthwhile institutions and to be involved in worthwhile pursuits and to try to be righteous?

Certainly that's not anything like the gross immorality, indecency, and sacrilege described in Galatians.

So why does Paul say he "has no confidence" in these things?

Because when we focus on natural relationships, on outward conformity, on human zeal and performance righteousness—even when involved in "good" activities—we miss the kind of life Christ offers us in the Spirit. We miss out on his life and peace—and we may even hold others back from experiencing that life and peace. That's the real reason focusing on the flesh produces nothing but "death."

To focus on the spiritual is to focus on the opposite of all the "good" but distracting things. It is a focus on:

- the spiritual supernatural,
- inward transformation,
- holy passion that comes from intimacy with God, and
- faith righteousness which comes by relationship with God rather than performance for God.

That's the kind of focus that's really worth finding in the interest of "life and peace." In the next four chapters, therefore, we will explore the deeper implications of focusing on the Spirit instead of the flesh.

CHAPTER

6 Living in the Shadows

WHEN SPEAKING TO A GROUP recently about flesh and spirit, I used an overhead projector to project shadows on a large screen. I placed an object on the projector and then asked my audience to identify that object from its shadow.

The results were interesting.

First, I placed a coin on the projector. After a few missed guesses, the audience properly identified it as a coin, but they could not tell me its denomination nor the year it was minted.

Next, I placed a bottle cap on the projector. They correctly identified it as such, but could not tell what its color was or what brand of drink it had capped.

Finally, I placed an object on the projector that everyone could identify immediately. They all eagerly stated that it was a safety pin and confidently speculated that it was made out of metal. Then I reached down and crumpled it up… it was only a piece of paper cut in the form of a safety pin.

The point? Shadows can only give you limited facts about reality. They can *point to* reality by giving information about the general shape of the object, but it's dangerous to try to determine all the facts about something by just looking at its shadow. To understand reality, you must see the substance, not just the shadow.

In the same way, as we choose to set our mind on the spiritual as opposed to the natural, we must understand the relationship of shadows and substance in the revelation of truth.

SHADOWS OF THE REAL THING

We begin with the realization that God has revealed himself in history. He did this first through natural, physical "shadows" that pointed to a spiritual substance and then through the revelation of the Substance itself in physical form.

The central figure of all biblical history is Jesus. He is the sum of all spiritual goodness—the fullness of the Godhead—incarnated in natural, physical form. As a result, those who are going to perceive life as it really is must see it by embracing Jesus as the Substance of every shadow of revelation. He must be allowed to interpret all the shadows that point toward him.

The Jews of the Old Testament we were shown many shadows that pointed toward the reality of Jesus and God's plan for them and the world.

The blood on the Israelite doorposts when they were in Egypt was a shadow. So was the blood of animal sacrifices offered as sin offerings. The substance was the blood of Jesus shed for our redemption.

When the children of Israel were in the wilderness and were being bitten by snakes, they were told by God to put a serpent on a pole. If they would look at the serpent, they would be healed. That serpent was a shadow; the substance was Jesus on a cross.

God met with Moses on Mount Sinai and gave him the law. What Moses brought down was a shadow of righteousness in the form of the Ten Commandments. Jesus is the substance of righteousness.

God instituted the priesthood for Israel. It was a shadow of the eternal intercession of Jesus Christ the Lord.

The temple of Solomon was a shadow of the body of Christ.

The nation of Israel was a shadow pointing toward the nation of believers who were to be God's eternal people.

HUNG UP ON THE SHADOWS

Notice that all these shadows are useful and important. They help us understand some things about spiritual reality; they give us clues as to what the substance is like. The problem comes when we forget that *shadows are not the substance.*

The Christians of Colossae in Paul's day did this, for example, when they got too hung up on the observance of particular worship rites and rituals. The apostle Paul admonished them: "Let no one act as your judge in regard to food or drink or in respect to a festival or a new moon or a Sabbath day—things which are a mere shadow of what is to come; but the substance belongs to Christ" (Col 2:16). Does the Colossians' situation sound familiar? Of course.

Religious people still argue about celebrating the Sabbath. You've heard the arguments: Saturday or Sunday? Morning or evening—or both? You've heard the bickering over what kind of rituals to observe: Formal or informal? Organs or guitars—or no instrument at all? Wine or grape juice? Religious people even get drawn into contests over what the righteous should eat (meat?), drink (caffeine? alcohol?), and wear (jeans? makeup? clerical collars?).

And all of these are arguments about shadows. When we allow ourselves to get caught up in them, our focus inevitably shifts from the spiritual to the point that we can see only the natural. We lose sight of the fact that God has always done things in the spiritual, and his people have always been essentially a spiritual people.

This shift of focus is exactly what happened to a group of Jews who became upset over Paul's preaching in the temple. (See Acts 21:28.) They accused him of speaking against "our people," "the Law," and "this place."

But why were these people so upset? Was he really preaching against them as a people or against their law or against the temple?

The answer, obviously, is no.

First, Paul spoke frequently about the strong loyalty he felt toward his people. He even wrote that he would risk his own damnation just to ensure the salvation of his fellow Israelites: "For I could wish that I myself were accursed, separated from Christ for the sake of my brethren, my kinsmen according to the flesh" (Rom 9:3).

Clearly, Paul desired more than anything that his natural kinsmen could be saved. It's obvious he was not against the Jewish people. Paul's point was simply that the natural Jew is not the central issue in God's plan. The natural Jews—the physical descendants of Abraham—are not the final nation of God. Instead, the nation of God has always been a people of faith—Abraham's *spiritual* descendants. (See Galatians 3:6-8; 4:21-30; Romans 9:6-8.) Faith—not genealogy—is the birthmark of God's people.

The physical nation of Israel was chosen by God to be a shadow—to point toward what the spiritual people of God were to be like. But the Jews of Paul's day refused to see this; that's why they accused Paul of preaching against "our people."

The second thing the Jews accused Paul of preaching against was the Jewish law—the law of Moses. But this was clearly not true. Paul repeatedly stressed that the law is righteous and holy and good and will never be abolished. But he also stressed that the *purpose* of the law is to expose the spiritual reality of human sin; it was never intended to make people righteous.

The law can only describe to us patterns of external behavior that correspond with inner righteousness. But Jesus came to show us the essence of righteousness—the spiritual reality that far transcends the letter of the law. Anyone who believes that righteousness is only some behavioral pattern has given his life to shadows, not substance.

The third accusation the Jews made against Paul was that he preached against the temple. He obviously wasn't, but he did say that the temple in Jerusalem was not God's holy place. If you want to find God's holy place, look at the church, the living body of God's people. Paul, along with his colleague, Peter, said it was built of living stones, with Jesus himself being the chief cornerstone (Eph 2:19-22; Col 1:24-27; 1 Pt 2:4-7).

In its day, Solomon's temple expressed the majesty and glory of God in a physical way. The church is to manifest the glory of God through its members for the rest of eternity. But it is just as foolish for us today to honor our buildings and believe that they are holy as it is for the Jews to look for the rebuilding of the temple.

The focus of history is not what is going to happen on a physical hill in Jerusalem, but what is happening on the hill of Zion which is the spiritual Jerusalem in the church of the living God. "But you have come to Mount Zion and to the city of the living God, the heavenly Jerusalem, and to myriads of angels, to the general assembly and church of the first-born who are enrolled in heaven, and to God, the Judge of all, and to the spirits of righteous men made perfect, and to Jesus, the mediator of a new covenant, and to the sprinkled blood, which speaks better than the blood of Abel" (Heb 12:22-24).

A GLIMPSE BEYOND THE SHADOWS

We, like Abraham, are looking for a spiritual city, not a physical one (Heb 11:10). We are people of the Spirit. We have come to realize that the invisible spiritual world is not only real, but it actually controls the more apparent physical world. We must refuse to live only in shadows, and we cannot afford to allow those who only see shadows to determine reality for us.

At the same time, we can give thanks for shadows. We can be grateful that a God who understands our limited perspective chooses to reveal his spiritual reality again and again in his physical creation. That's why he persisted, over the entire sweep of history, in giving us shadows that point toward his spiritual reality. That's why he continues to make himself known not only through the promptings of the Spirit in our lives, but also through his creation and through other people.

Most of all, that's why, at the crux of history, the spiritual reality at the center of the universe actually took on natural, physical form. In Jesus, flesh and Spirit intersect. In him, natural and spiritual reality combine. And that's why, when we keep our eyes and hearts centered on him and his grace, we have the best chance of keeping all our shadows in perspective.

CHAPTER

7 Dedicated to Being Right

IT REALLY ISN'T ANY FUN living around a perfectionist. Such a person is destined to be unhappy because the world is imperfect. Yet some have interpreted religion to be the solution to imperfection and have tried to be right by doing right.

Let me assure you the God of the gospel has more in mind for you than demanding that you "shape up"—that you do the right thing and make sure that others do right as well. He sent Jesus to find you, transform you from the inside out and release you to live in the invisible kingdom of God while still in the physical world.

Set that firmly in mind: Jesus didn't come to judge you. In fact, he loves you enough to change you.

The perfectionist mentality, in fact, is just another part of the deadly "flesh perspective." Any time we choose this mindset, we are forced to live a life of outward conformity that generally takes two forms: (1) an inordinate emphasis on *total conformity* to the guidelines of a particular group and (2) a narrow focus on *correct doctrine* as defined by the leaders who interpret truth to a particular group.

A PERVERTED DEDICATION

The perverted sense of dedication that inhabits the mind that is set on the flesh is defined in terms of meticulous obedience to the letter of the law, with little regard to healthy relationships. It was precisely this way of thinking that Jesus encountered one day when he went home to eat lunch with a Pharisee.

Upon reaching the Pharisee's house, Jesus went in and immediately reclined at the table. When the Pharisee observed this, he expressed surprise that Jesus had not ceremoniously washed his hands and utensils before the meal. It was in this context that Jesus spoke some of the most scathing words about the mentality of the Pharisees:

> "Now you Pharisees clean the outside of the cup and of the platter; but inside of you, you are full of robbery and wickedness. You foolish ones, did not he who made the outside make the inside also?... Woe to you, Pharisees! For you pay tithe of mint and rue and every kind of garden herb, and yet disregard justice and the love of God; but these are the things you should have done without neglecting the others. Woe to you, Pharisees! For you love the front seats in the synagogues, and the respectful greetings in the market places. Woe to you! For you are like concealed tombs, and the people who walk over them are unaware of it." **Lk 11:39-44**

Jesus was not criticizing the Jewish ceremonial laws, of course. He was attacking the mindset that won't settle for anything short of total conformity to a set of rules and regulations.

When any mentality insists on this kind of complete conformity, there has to be a way of measuring compliance. Everybody must do all the externals properly and uniformly. Unfortunately, this easily leads to ignoring the more important inner reality.

The Pharisees were highly insulted that Jesus did not wash his hands properly, but they were not insulted at all by their own hatred of their fellow man. Jesus said this is not only an invalid perspective, but a dangerous one, for it gives those watching a false sense of reality. The heroes of righteousness become those who best conform to their agreed-upon rules, while those who are actually expressing the true life of God may be rejected or even killed because of their nonconformity.

THE PARTY LINE

Along with this misguided emphasis on complete dedication often comes the inordinate focus on correct doctrine as defined by the legalists. If conformity is important, then correct doctrine is a primary issue. After all, we must know what issues are the basis of our uniformity.

Correct doctrine is an emphasis on believing all the right truths in the right way and saying them with the right words. It is a focus on right answers, regardless of bad attitudes. And once again, it will inevitably sacrifice the individual for the sake of the institution. The written code will ultimately replace God as the object of worship.

If we spent the rest of our lives giving thanks to God for the revelation and preservation of the Scriptures, we could never thank him too much. But there are many today who, because of their focus on outward conformity, have made the Scriptures into something that God never intended; they have made them a god in themselves. Jesus himself said that the Scriptures "testify of me." Yet some have elevated the Scriptures to such a point that Jesus himself seems only an addendum to them.

Only Jesus himself is the living Word of God. The Scriptures testify of him. They must be read, appreciated, and appropriated, but they are never to take the place of the living Word of God.

Obviously, doctrine is important. The word *doctrine* simply means teaching. And Jesus was the epitome of the teacher of truth. The problem comes when those who stress the correct doctrine lose sight of the *reason* behind the doctrine—when they become preoccupied with the right answers to the exclusion of the right attitude.

THE LETTER OR THE SPIRIT OF THE LAW

In Luke 10 we read about how a lawyer, seeking to put Jesus to the test, came up and questioned him: "Teacher, what shall I do to inherit eternal life?"

Jesus said, "What's written in the law? How does it read to you?"

The lawyer answered, "You shall love the Lord your God with all your heart, and with all your soul, and with all your strength, and with all your mind; and your neighbor as yourself."

And Jesus responded, "You've answered correctly."

The lawyer had scored 100 percent on his test of biblical interpretation. His doctrine was right. The problem was, he did not possess the life of the Spirit necessary to live out his doctrine. So when Jesus added, "Do this, and you will live," the man felt threatened and began trying to justify himself.

"And who is my neighbor?" he asked—obviously looking for an out.

In response to his question, Jesus told the story that vividly pictured the difference between the letter of correct doctrine and spiritual reality behind the teaching.

You know the story, of course. A man fell among robbers while traveling from Jerusalem to Jericho. The thieves stripped him and beat him and left him half dead. And while he lay there moaning, several people passed him on the road. First, a priest came along and spotted the injured man, but passed by on the other side of the road. Likewise, a Levite saw the man and passed by on the other side. Then, finally, a Samaritan came by. Taking compassion for the injured man, he bandaged his wounds, took him to the inn, and paid for the man's recovery at the inn.

Now to understand fully the impact of this story, you have to realize that the Samaritans were a half-breed people, despised by the Jews. Jesus himself had said that some of their theology was wrong. Do you remember when Jesus talked to the woman by the well in Samaria? She asked Jesus, "We worship in one mountain and you worship in another. Who's to know who is right?" And Jesus essentially said to her that the Jews were right; the Samaritans were wrong (Jn 4:22).

So Jesus was setting up a very uncomfortable comparison for the young lawyer. "Who followed the law better, Jesus was asking, "the doctrinally correct but uncaring priest and Levite, or the half-breed with a faulty theology and a compassionate heart?" The shame-faced lawyer had to answer that the "neighbor"—the one who best lived out the spirit of the law —was not the one who held correct doctrine, but the one who showed mercy (Lk 10:25-37, my paraphrase).

RIGHT DOCTRINE, WRONG ATTITUDE

Now please, I would never suggest that we stamp approval on erroneous doctrine. It is absolutely essential that we believe the basics. But the basics are not all that many. And the issues that normally cause division are not usually the basics at all. They are the nonessential teachings around which people gather to find their own identity.

Any teaching that does not fit with the words of Jesus and does not lead to godly living—living that correlates to the character of God in Christ Jesus—is false teaching. (See 1 Timothy 6:3-4.) And even a right doctrine approached with the wrong attitude becomes, in the heart, an expression of wrong doctrine.

When I first went to college, I could hardly wait to go to my first meeting of the ministerial association, an organization that provided fellowship to those studying for the ministry. At one of my first meetings, however, an upperclassman came to me, looked me sternly in the face and said, "How is your eschatology?"

Now, I had grown up in a small, rural church in the South where we never used a lot of big theological terms. So, here I was a freshman at the university, wanting to appear bright and well-read, and I had honestly never heard the word *eschatology*. It sounded a lot like a skin rash to me. I did not know how to respond!

I thought perhaps I could fake it with him, and so I responded, "Mine's fine. How's yours?"

He did not think that was amusing at all. He said, "What I'm asking you is, in your view of the Second Coming, are you premillennial, postmillennial, or amillennial?"

In his effort to clarify the situation for me, he had only muddied the waters of my mind. I not only did not know what eschatology was, I had never heard the terms *premillennial, postmillennial,* or *amillennial.* And so, stalling for time, I just opened my mouth and said, "Ahhhh..." He honestly thought I was giving an answer and was declaring myself to be an "aah-millennialist," to which he replied, "I thought so. You look like a liberal. I knew it when I first saw you."

The rest of my days at school, this person believed I was a liberal. If the truth were known, I was probably one of the more theologically conservative men in school at the time.

Now, I dare not judge that upperclassman because I, too, have had times when I was so deceived by the focus on personal doctrinal viewpoints that I have lost sight of the more important underlying spiritual issues. My point is, I would have been much better off if that other young man had offered to encourage me as an ignorant freshman seeking to find acceptance and fellowship among the brethren. In fact, the whole world would be better off if we focused a little less on getting all our doctrinal ducks in a row and a lot more on internalizing the righteousness of God—showing mercy, compassion, and unfeigned love from a pure heart.

CHOOSING LIFE OVER "RIGHT"

I never cease to be amazed at the ridiculous interpretations that people's minds can conjure up when they are, in fact, blind to the essence of life. One of my favorite stories is the one where the Sadducees were trying to trick Jesus. They did not believe in the doctrine of resurrection and were trying to prove to Jesus how absurd it was to believe in life after death. So they told him a hypothetical story about a woman whose husband died childless. The dead man's brother married the woman but then also died, leaving no children. This happened six times.

The Sadducees asked Jesus, "When this woman gets to heaven, whose wife will she be?" And they fully expected Jesus to be stumped. Their limited minds remained so tightly focused on the flesh that their interpretation of Scripture was absolutely absurd.

Jesus' response to them is his eternal response to the fleshly mentality: "You are mistaken, not understanding the Scriptures, or the power of God" (Mt 22:29).

The fact is, those who are unwilling to know the power of God will never truly know the Scriptures—for the Scriptures attest to the vitality of the living Christ. When we appropriate them in our lives, the Scriptures become expressions of the life of Christ on earth. But when the Scriptures become an end in themselves—and especially when they are used to beat others over the head—they're not only useless in the life of a believer, they become deadly.

If the Bible is death to us, where can we find life? If God's revelation of himself through the sacred Scriptures is shut off, where shall we find hope? This is the plight of the person whose mind is set on flesh. Such a mentality can seem so right with its focus on conforming to the "righteous norm." Religious activities and holy-sounding words can fool some who watch, but the inner sense of fatigue, frustration, and failure is unbearable. The "life and peace" mentioned by Paul seems unattainable until we cry out for mercy.

But the good news is: mercy is available. There is an alternative to the fleshly mindset. And grace is available even when we just can't manage to conform to the rules and get our doctrine exactly straight.

CHAPTER

8 Sitting Down Inside

A FEW YEARS AGO I was praying about how to raise up leaders in the church. I asked the Lord, "How do I know when someone has the makings of a leader?" As I began writing down my thoughts, the Lord responded: "No one is ready to lead until he or she has sat down inside."

What does that mean? Simply that the best and most effective leaders are those who have ceased striving and entered into rest with Jesus. Their sense of debt has taken on deeper dimensions than guilt could ever produce. They feel a sense of obligation to every person who has not heard the good news of Jesus, but it is a positive obligation. There is no oppression, there is no striving or labor—just love looking for expression. Most of all, their zeal for causes has been swallowed by a passion for intimacy with God.

A CAUSE IS NOT ENOUGH

I can remember, as a teenager, belting out the words to "The Impossible Dream" and being sure that I, too, was willing to "march into hell for a heavenly cause." And I was not unique. Every generation has its own crusades, and many causes call to us.

More often than not, in fact, our heroes are people who personify zeal. Our society honors those who are prepared to make sacrifices or even give their lives for the sake of their cause—be it defending their country or supporting the arts or feeding the hungry or fighting crime.

With that as background, let me make a statement that may surprise you: *A person who dies for a cause only, no matter how great the cause, has paid too great a price.* To put it another way, a person who gives his or her life for a cause has misjudged the value of his life and the cause.

There is only one thing worth giving your life for, and that is a *relationship* motivated by love. Love does not look for causes; it looks for persons.

Jesus was a full expression of God on the earth. He did not die for a cause, he died for love. When Jesus was praying in the garden, the issue was not the principle for which he was dying, but his relationship with God the Father. He died not to prove anything, but to obey his Father's will.

The big turnaround in the apostle Paul's life came when he switched from a cause to a relationship. Before, he had been controlled by a human zeal—the persecution of the fledgling church. He had been committed to a cause he believed was right, but obviously he was not motivated by the life of God. And then, Paul encountered Jesus on the road to Damascus. He sat down inside and backed off from causes. From that point onward, everything he did grew out of the relationship that had changed his life.

THE PITFALLS OF ZEAL

Am I making too much of this distinction between causes and relationships? I don't think so. As I see it, cause-oriented behavior carries with it several inherent dangers.

Pitfall #1: Wrong Motivations. First of all, a zeal for a cause is, more likely than not, motivated by anger. Over the long run, anger-driven behavior will not produce godly results.

All of us are aware of things around us that are out of kilter in the world. When things are not going right, something inside of us wants to lash out at this violated justice—to "fix things" by annihilating all the injustices that are around. For instance, I could very easily get caught up in fighting abortion, child abuse, pornography, gambling, drugs, and so on. Seeing the pain that these practices bring into the world stirs me up; I want to do something about them.

But if my involvement in fighting those vices and abuses is motivated by human anger, then it is doomed to failure over the long run. I may make some headway and achieve some success at furthering my cause, but eventually I will succumb to burnout or bitterness or corruption.

The Bible says, "the anger of man does not achieve the righteousness of God" (Jas 1:20). And the history of even "worthy" causes of the centuries backs up that reality.

Please understand, however, that I am talking about motivation, not about the actions themselves. I am not saying we should condone the evils around us—or simply hide our heads in the sand. There may well be times when we need to speak out against injustice and work to help others. We may even be called to be leaders in ending abuses and carrying out works of justice and mercy.

But—and this is a crucial difference—if we do any of these things simply out of human anger (or out of any other motivation besides love), our work will not produce the righteousness of God. And this will be true even though the world may accept our motives, applaud our deeds, or even record us in history as martyrs or world changers.

Pitfall #2: Factionalism. A second pitfall of cause-oriented behavior is its tendency to split people into factions. People gather around angry, zealous leaders because almost everyone has a feeling of being disenfranchised. In fact, some people become leaders in the first place because they are able to enunciate their anger more forcefully than others and, therefore, become spokesmen for everybody else who is simply angry.

As people gather around different leaders, indignation tends to be magnified. Divisions develop. Factions are exposed. And the predictable result is ongoing strife and enmity. If it happens within the body of Christ, God's people are once again unnecessarily divided.

It has often been said that causes unite people. A look at the history of causes—"worthy" and "unworthy"—will show that the opposite more often is true. Love unites people. Causes divide people. Think of the murder and hatred done on behalf of causes through the centuries. And this happened even in the church, when religious people killed their brothers and sisters over the cause of "pure" doctrine.

Now, once again, I am talking more about motivation than action—more about what goes on inside us than about the external results. Even when we act out of love and a relationship with Christ, there will be times when we experience strife. Carrying out God's will does not guarantee us harmony with the people around us. Acting out of love and relationship, however, does promise us inner peace and harmony that enable us to be peacemakers in the world rather than rabble-rousers. Causes—even good causes—cannot make that promise.

Pitfall #3: Misplaced Passion. The third inherent danger in cause-oriented behavior is that the cause tends to displace God as the primary object of worship. God has deposited in the heart of each human being a passion for intimacy with him. When we expend that passion on some cause, we rob both ourselves and God of the intimacy he designed for us to experience.

We are all too often guilty of building with our hands what we lack in our hearts. I've known men and women who spent huge amounts of money and energy to create a peaceful environment—a garden, a den, a cabin by the lake—as a substitute for the inner peace they lack. In the same way, many who can't or won't focus their God-given passion for intimacy on God will develop zeal for a cause. But just as building a peaceful environment cannot by itself bring peace to a restless and conflicted heart, a misplaced passion cannot ever really bring us satisfaction.

Pitfall #4: Bad Timing. Fourth, a zeal for causes tends to call us into action prematurely.

If Jesus had been listening to the call of a cause when he was twelve years old, he would certainly have started his ministry at that point. It is obvious that he knew there was something terribly wrong with the "religious setup" around him. Even the religious leaders of his day were ignorant of the Father's business, while he was acutely aware of it. The cause of unredeemed humanity would surely have drawn him into ministry at age twelve. Yet, because he was not called by a cause, he was able to rest for approximately eighteen more years and begin his ministry only when his growing relationship with his Father assured him that the time was right.

The road of Christian service is littered with the burned-out, broken bodies of those who gave their all prematurely—and who gave it to a cause instead of a relationship.

I believe, for example, that today's church is paying the price for worshiping at the altar of youth. Youth is wonderful and energetic, but its great danger is to operate in human zeal rather than in divine passion. While age does not automatically make one wiser, it does provide a longer opportunity to distinguish between that which is human and that which is divine.

Certainly there are worthy causes. Surely those of us who love God hate such things as abortion, pornography, child abuse, corruption in government, misuse of drugs, and so on. All of us want to see the hungry fed, the grieving comforted, the sick healed. But none of these causes in themselves call us into action. We must believe that the Lord himself is more interested in all of these than we are. There is the fullness of time in which assignments are made and proper people are put in the proper place. If Jesus, the very Son of God, was willing to wait to be assigned by divine love, then certainly it cannot be wrong for us to sit down inside and wait for our divine assignment.

GETTING OUR FOCUS CLEAR

All these pitfalls make it clear that the key to a satisfying and meaningful life is not zeal for a cause but a passion for a person. And not just any person. The key to effective leadership is not rallying people around a cause, but sitting down inside and getting to know God. Once we do that, we are ready to take action—but with totally different motivations and vastly different results.

Paul made that clear in 2 Corinthians 5:13: "If we are beside ourselves, it is for God" and in Philippians 3:8, when he stated his number-one priority: "I count all things to be loss in view of the surpassing value of knowing Christ Jesus my Lord."

Knowing Christ is, of course, the key to developing a divine passion. A person who knows Jesus will love Jesus. It's as simple as that. To know him is to love him. I would say to you, simply and directly, that if you don't love him it is because you have not taken the time to know him. Out of that intimacy of knowledge and love will grow a consummation of relationship that produces fruit, just as a bride and bridegroom enter into intimacy and children are produced.

A few years ago a book was published that sold thousands of copies because it predicted the Second Coming of Christ in 1988. The subject of the book was "88 Reasons Why the Lord Will Return in '88." I was astounded at the uproar that this little book caused. For centuries people have discussed the Second Coming, debated the Second Coming, predicted the Second Coming, and argued over the events of the Second Coming.

Now, let me state clearly that I personally believe Jesus is coming again. But there is something about all the hoopla over the Second Coming that bothers me. If I read the apostle Paul correctly, it is not the *event* that turned him on, but the *Person* who was coming.

Too often today I hear the Second Coming talked about as an event—a happening that is going to get us out of our mess, relieve us of our troubles, and set us free from our predicaments. But I am more interested in the coming of *Jesus* than in the "Second Coming"; to me, the event is secondary to the person. The wonderful thing is that while I wait for his physical return, I can enjoy intimacy with him every day.

ENERGIZED BY LOVE

Now, once again, please don't misunderstand. The cure for cause-oriented behavior is obviously not passivity and laziness. Sitting down inside is not the same thing as doing nothing. As God's people, we are part of God's redemptive plan in the earth. Everything that the Enemy has stolen will one day be restored, and we have the privilege of being a part of that restoration process.

But the point here is, it is a fleshly focus to concentrate on human zeal when the Spirit is focusing on divine passion. Divine passion will take us further than human zeal can imagine. It will produce greater fruit and do it without sweat. It is that divine energy which propels one through obstacles in a quest for the object of its love.

It's a simple fact: Causes require more resources than they create. When people are motivated by zeal, they can never produce the amount of energy required to complete the task. Again, we are familiar with the cries for help from those who have given themselves to fulfill a mission or a dream. When they run a little short of money or a little short of energy or commitment, their tendency is to create a larger cause to create more anger, thus more resources.

It happens on a national level, too. In the past we have had to portray the communists as bigger than they really were, the devil as bigger than he really is, the situation worse than we first had thought. All this to get people stirred up so their anger will release enough resources to get the job done.

But here's another simple fact: Love has enough energy to accomplish the task it has been called to do. Love will never find itself without enough resources, because "love never fails" (1 Cor 13:8). When we sit down inside, we receive his love fully, and then we are energized to go where he wants us to go.

When Jesus was talking to Peter by the Sea of Galilee after the crucifixion and resurrection, he asked, "Peter, do you love me?" And Peter responded in the affirmative as best he could. Then Jesus repeated the question. Three times he told Peter to "Feed my sheep."

Now, I find it interesting that Jesus never said to Peter, "Do you care about sheep? Are you concerned about the plight of hungry sheep?" He did not want Peter committed to the cause of finding and feeding sheep; he wanted Peter committed to him. Out of a commitment of love would come a directive and an expenditure of energy that would accomplish the goal of establishing the church.

The passion that must control our life must be a passion for relationship with God himself. It comes out of sitting down inside and learning to know him and depend on him. But then, out of that relationship, we will receive assignments from him so that we find our proper place of service in the body of Christ. And out of our continued relationship with him will come the energy we need to complete our assigned tasks.

Once we look at our Christian lives from this vantage point, the concept of "holy living" takes on a whole new color. Much of the church has been content to settle for a "disciplined" life and call it holiness. We have assumed that if we use our time wisely, read our Bibles, pray, witness, tithe, and so on, then we are holy. But we can work hard at all those pursuits and still reap nothing but boredom and burnout.

As a reaction to that kind of spiritual nonproductivity, the word *radical* has been used to motivate people to get more involved. The word *radical*, however, creates mental pictures of someone doing something beyond the norm of their behavior. When I think of radical behavior, I think of doing something that I would not ordinarily do out of my innermost being, but something to prove that I am really serious about an issue.

But divine passion is something quite different from either wearying discipline or wild-eyed radicalism. Instead of wearing us out or "pumping us up," a passion for God releases energy in our lives.

THE POWER OF PASSION

Passion releases energy in our lives, while a lack of passion drains us of energy. Have you ever been around someone who had no passion for anything? It's very difficult to talk to such people. You ask them where they work, and with a humdrum monotone they say something like "Oh, I work down at the factory five days a week." You ask them about their family, and in a barely audible murmur they tell how many kids they have and how old they are. You ask them about their hobbies, and they have to scratch their head as they try to think of anything they've done except work, eat, sleep, burp, and go out once in a while. There's no energy, no life, no fun.

On the other hand, I'm sure you've had the experience of talking to someone who is very quiet in the conversation until you mention something for which they have a passion. It may be fishing or painting or collecting bottle caps, but it's something that releases energy inside of them.

Often, when I travel somewhere to minister, someone will be assigned as my guide. I find this a fun opportunity to get to know someone new, so I usually try to find out what interests my guide, what makes him or her tick. Occasionally, however, I run into someone in whom I cannot find that spark of interest. One such occasion occurred a few years ago.

An older man had volunteered for the task of driving me back and forth to my speaking engagements. All week I fruitlessly tried to discover the passion in his life. I asked him about his family and found out only mundane details. I asked him about his future and he only mumbled something about retirement. I had almost given up and concluded that this was truly a man without any passion when by chance I discovered that his hobby was pollinating tomatoes. When I asked him about that, his eyes lit up, and twenty years seem to fall off his tired body. For hours he explained to me all the things he had learned in growing his new breed of tomatoes.

Now, I had never wanted to be a tomato grower, but by the time that man was finished, I, too, was excited about tomatoes. Energy was swirling around in the car as he told me about his hobby.

That's true of us all. Once we discover a passion in life, life begins to flow. Energy begins to rise. Excitement dances in the air. You can tell the person is motivated from the inside. Energy is released not only in the person who has the passion, but also in those around him or her.

The negative side of this truth is that people who have no passion are very gullible and become susceptible to people who operate out of zeal for causes or misplaced passion. That's how crusaders and con artists get people to follow and support them.

In these strategic days I believe we will see many people, Christians included, become disillusioned and hurt because they lack their own passion and become caught up in the false dreams and futile causes of others. The financial empire-builder Donald Trump targeted this very danger when he wrote about himself (years before his empire began to crumble), "I play to people's fantasies. People may not always think big themselves but they can still get very excited by people who do.... People want to believe that something is the biggest and the greatest and the most spectacular."[1]

I say to you, if you do not have a passion of your own, you'll be susceptible to those who do have a passion. You could easily be carried off by the dreams of those whose passion may not come from God.

FAITH PRODUCES PASSION

As energy comes from passion, passion comes from faith. This is true of mere human faith or the higher-level biblical faith. But let's talk about biblical faith. When biblical faith is expressed, passion is released.

Look, for example, at Abraham and Sarah, two people whose bodies had grown too old to have children. They had no energy for reproduction. And yet, when they finally believed God's direct word to them, energy was released that rejuvenated their bodies and helped them to cooperate with God's plan. Once again they began planning to have children because there was energy in them, and that energy came from their faith.

Gideon is another example. He was facing the army of the Midianites, a military force much bigger than his little band of three hundred. But God allowed him to go down to the enemy camp and overhear a conversation that revealed God's plan and strategy for Gideon's battle. Faith then released in him an energy that not only motivated him but his whole army. This scared little band, which had nothing for war tools except pots and torches, were so energized by Gideon's expression of faith that they routed the enemy army.

Then there was Joshua, stewing about how he was to take Jericho. As he wandered around, he was confronted by an angel of the Lord who gave him God's message. And the moment he believed in that message, passion was released in

1. Donald Trump, *Trump: The Art of the Deal* (New York: Warner, 1987), 58.

him. As a result, he had the energy not only to encourage himself, but to motivate others to follow God's strange plan. How could a man get people to march around a city six days? It was because his belief led him to passion, and his passion released energy in those around him. The Israelites followed Joshua in marching around Jericho. On the seventh day they saw the walls fall down.

If biblical faith and divine passion are the keys to a worthwhile and fruitful life, how do we get the kind of biblical faith and passion? Faith is released when we hear the voice of God.

Maybe the greatest eternal fact that we need to know is that God will do what he says. When one personally hears the voice of God, there is an opportunity for faith. Until one has this personal encounter, there is no life-changing faith.

There are three basic areas where it's important that I hear God's personal word to me.

Chosen by God. First, I must hear in my inner being that I was chosen by God (Eph 1:13-14). When the revelation dawns in my spirit that I was chosen by God before I did anything right or wrong or made any choices on my own, an atmosphere of unconditional love is created that makes intimacy possible. Until this revelation comes, however, I am always wondering how my performance measures up to God's expectations.

Now, the natural mind has difficulty fathoming how God can select some without rejecting others. And yet biblical revelation never says that God has rejected anyone. Our minds must submit to the revelation of God in these matters. We must not judge God by our definition of fairness. You can be sure that there will be no one in heaven saying, "I wanted to go to hell, but I was chosen by God and he wouldn't let me." Nor will there be anyone in hell saying, "I wanted to go to heaven, and I asked Jesus to save me, but he wouldn't."

The point is, when it becomes clear in your spirit that God wanted you, chose you, without regard to your performance, all the pressure will be off. You will be able to enjoy the security of intimacy with him—and both faith and passion will be the result.

The prophet Jeremiah said that God's word was like "a burning fire shut up in my bones" (Jer 20:9). That's a beautiful description of passion. To Jeremiah it was something beyond his rational mind's ability to comprehend. The word of God was so much a part of his essence that he couldn't control it. It was in the very marrow of his bones.

And how did Jeremiah get such passion? It began when Jeremiah heard God say he was selected from his mother's womb. (See Jeremiah 1:5.) He had a sense of destiny, a sense of being special, eternally accepted by God. And this created an atmosphere in Jeremiah's life that was right for faith and for passion (Jer 1:4-10).

Commissioned by God. Another word Jeremiah received—the second necessity for all of us—was a special assignment from God. God told Jeremiah what he was to do. He gave him his call and his commission. Specifically, Jeremiah was to "pluck up and to break down, to destroy and to overthrow, to build and to plant." God would tell him what words to say and whom he was to say them to. He had a mission. (See Jeremiah 1:9-10.)

We see this same pattern in the apostle Paul (Gal 1:15-16). Paul realized he had been chosen before the foundation of the world and was set aside while still in his mother's womb to be a minister of the gospel. At his conversion, Paul received his call and commission and was told essentially what would happen to him for the rest of his life. Every Christian has a God-given right to know his call and commission.

Now, it is possible you may be feeling disenfranchised because you have not had a dramatic vision like Jeremiah's or a dramatic conversion like the apostle Paul's conversion. But remember that God speaks in many ways—in the still, small voice as well as in the fire and the whirlwind.

God could be speaking to you through the gifts he has

given to you and the trials he has let you walk through. He gave you a specific personality with specific gifts. He has placed specific truths into your life by allowing you to encounter situations that would test the mettle of your character.

It is important that you not make this matter of being called and commissioned too mystical. Believe it. God has an assignment for you. He is not reticent to share it with you. Possibly it is so obvious you are missing it. Ask God for eyes to see your assignment in the furthering of his kingdom.

Filled with His Power. The third reality that must come is the release of God's power through us. In other words, there must be an expectation in our hearts to see God work through us. Jesus said, "The works that I do shall [the believer] do also; and greater works than these shall he do; because I go to the Father" (Jn 14:12).

As we represent God in this world and speak in obedience to him, we should expect our words to have the force of his power behind them. When we pray for the sick, we should expect his healing to operate. When we speak to demons, we should expect God to enforce the authority he has given to us. Without this expectation, there will be little life in our activity. Jesus sent forth his disciples—and that includes us—with the same authority and power with which he came. It is our responsibility and privilege to believe that he is working through us and accomplishing his mighty purpose.

As we make being intimate with Jesus the priority of our life, we will find that we will have a revelation that we are chosen in him and special to him. We will also discover that we do have a calling and a commission, and enough faith will be released in us to believe that his power is working through us.

We are privileged to be a part of the great redemptive plan of the ages, bringing to pass the goals and purposes of the kingdom of God. For that reason, we must never settle for a cause. Zeal just won't cut it. Instead, we must sit down inside and let God develop in us the passion we need to live on a higher level. And, we can be sure, he won't disappoint us.

CHAPTER

9 Free from Me

THE REAL PRISONERS in life are those whose focus is on themselves. They are constantly evaluating, analyzing, criticizing, and justifying their actions and attitudes. When they have achieved certain standards, they are confident, but they are insecure when they haven't performed the way they think they should. Periodically they get depressed even when they haven't "failed" at anything they know of. This is the journey of the self-righteous.

"But I'm not self-righteous," you may protest. "I know how bad I am. I would never boast of being anything close to perfect." But self-righteousness doesn't really mean thinking you are perfect. Self-righteousness is simply self-consciousness that is trying to live up to the anticipated expectations of God.

Self-righteousness shows itself in a search for one's own identity apart from relationship. Identity is sought in performance, position, and success. But let's face it, you will never have an identity except in your relationship with Jesus. In Christ you are important. Outside of him, you are lost.

If you are looking for your own individual identity, you will forever be self-conscious—always conscious of your performance and your failure, always regretting that you didn't do better or gloating over the fact that you did pretty well after all. You will be acutely aware of other people's failures, so you will constantly battle judgmentalism. And you will be very alert to how you are perceived by others, so you will struggle with the fear of rejection and a people-pleasing spirit.

But what's the alternative? The apostle Paul distinguished between self-righteousness and faith-righteousness; in Philippians 3 he speaks of "not having a righteousness of my own derived from the Law, but that which is through faith in Christ, the righteousness which comes from God on the basis of faith."

Faith-righteousness brings us into a consciousness of our relationship with God, not our performance for God. A consciousness of his performance is much more liberating than a consciousness of our own performance.

Faith righteousness also produces in me the ability to be comfortable with my weaknesses. I realize that I am a clay vessel in which his glory shines. (See 2 Corinthians 4:6-7.) I am not expected to perform perfectly; in fact, God's strength shows through my weakness. He gets the glory, and I get his peace.

REDEFINING RIGHTEOUSNESS

The unaided, natural mind will always define righteousness in terms of knowing good in order to do it and knowing evil in order to avoid it. As a result, righteousness will always be thought of in terms of restrictions, regulations, and requirements.

Jesus turned that idea of righteousness on its ear. When the inquisitive lawyer came up to Jesus and asked him what was the greatest commandment, Jesus summed up all of Scripture in a simple, profound statement: "to love God... and your neighbor as yourself." In essence, Jesus was redefining righteousness in terms of *relationship*, not in terms of requirements. That kind of righteousness is precisely what Paul later described as "righteousness which comes from God on the basis of faith."

Once we start looking at righteousness in terms of faith and relationships rather than keeping rules and regulations, a lot of other ideas begin shifting as well. For example, redefining righteousness will also redefine sin for us.

It is obviously no fun for anyone to live with a continual sin-consciousness (which is just another form of self-consciousness). I really feel sorry for those who go to bed each night certain that they have committed thousands of conscious and unconscious sins. It's so unnecessary; we can be sure that our Father is more concerned with our being free from the ravages of sin than we are.

One of the reasons we live with such a sin-consciousness is that we persist in thinking of sin, like righteousness, in terms of rules rather than relationships. We have defined sin as legal violations rather than as mishandled relationships.

But that's not the way Jesus looked at sin. When Jesus was explaining the ministry of the Holy Spirit who was to come after his ascension, he said, "And He, when He comes, will convict the world concerning sin... *because they do not believe in me*" (Jn 16:8-9, emphasis mine). Notice that Jesus was speaking of sin as the violation of a trust relationship, not the breaking of legal standards. The heart of all sin is unbelief, mistrust, or neglect of a faith relationship.

Looking at sin and righteousness in terms of relationships rather than regulations can really change the way we approach life. For let's face it: breaking a law doesn't have the same effect on me as breaking a heart.

If I'm driving down the highway and notice the speedometer is a little above the speed limit, I don't immediately go into deep grief over the fact that I've broken the law and thereby proven to be unrighteous. I may let up on the gas pedal a bit, but if the truth were really known, I do it more out of a desire not to get a ticket or not to have a wreck than out of a desire not to break the law.

However, I have noticed that hurting someone I care about does break my heart. I have found that I will go far beyond the demands of the law in order to keep from hurting my relationship with my wife or my children or my friends.

Our culture has hundreds of rules about being a good husband: earn a good living, be home for dinner, remember anniversaries, and so on. Failing to keep those rules doesn't necessarily break my heart. But when I fail to build up my wife and encourage her in her own journey, then my heart is broken.

RELATIONSHIP SECURES SALVATION

This "rules versus relationship" view of sin and righteousness even extends to the deepest issues of salvation and eternal security. There are thousands of well-meaning Christians who live each day in doubt over whether they are "really saved." The problem with many of them is they are focused on "Did I do it right?" They are not sure they prayed the right prayer or prayed with enough sincerity. Or they wonder if they knew enough when they decided to follow Christ to make that decision properly. (I have heard many say, "After all, I was only ten years old. I couldn't have known enough about God to make a proper decision." But if you were fifty years old, you would not have known enough to make such a decision!)

Some people who grew up in the faith may even have trouble pointing to a specific moment of coming to Christ; they simply felt it was time to make their growing relationship with him public. And then, later, they wonder whether they somehow skipped an important step.

The point is, the assurance of salvation comes from our confidence in God's faithfulness and our relationship with him, not from our confidence in doing things right.

I had a wonderful experience some time back. I was speaking to a church in Florida when a young woman came up for conversation. She said, "Would you mind talking to me for a few minutes? Several years ago I had an accident, and I have amnesia. Every once in a while I will see something that looks familiar, and pursuing that feeling further sometimes helps my memory. You look very familiar to me, and I wondered if somewhere in the past we might have met."

I was happy to talk with her for awhile, for she had great joy and peace about her countenance.

"When did you have your accident?" I inquired.

"About five years ago," she replied.

"And when did you come to know the Lord?" I asked.

"About twelve years ago."

"Oh... you mean you came to know the Lord, and since then you've lost your memory?"

"Yes," she said.

"Well then, how do you know for sure that you're saved? You can't remember the prayer you prayed or the events surrounding your conversion, right?"

She answered, "That's exactly right. But Mr. Hall, I know I'm saved because I love Jesus."

Although I couldn't help that young woman regain her memory, she helped me regain an appreciation for a salvation based on relationship.

Now, I'm not saying that it is unimportant to remember the conversion experience. I'm not saying it's unimportant actually to invite Jesus into our lives at a particular time (although some people may have difficulty pinpointing the specific moment when this happened). What I am saying is that God's emphasis on righteousness focuses not on right actions (even "religious" actions), but on right relationship.

"Well then, how can I know I'm saved?" someone might ask. We can settle that right now. Are you trusting Jesus as your Savior and as Lord of your life? "Yes, but I don't know if I prayed the right prayer or if I was sincere enough... or if I can even pinpoint when I accepted him as Savior." That is not the issue. The issue with God is your relationship with him now.

RELATIONSHIP STIMULATES REPENTANCE AND FORGIVENESS

Relationship is also the key to grasping how God's grace and forgiveness really work. For our common misunderstandings of righteousness and sin color our understandings of forgiveness.

I spoke recently to a woman who related her heartbreaking story to me. Just a few short months before, her husband had left her for his younger secretary, leaving her with two small children to raise alone.

"He was a Christian," the wife lamented. "a leader in the church. And do you know what really bothers me? I'm afraid that now he is just going to say he's sorry, repent, and everything is going to be okay. Does that sound right to you?"

Her question is a legitimate one. Can someone flaunt his or her own selfish ways in God's face and then simply rectify the situation by saying, "I'm sorry. I was wrong"? If our definition of sin is that someone has violated the laws of God and our understanding of grace is that God just forgives him or her those violations, then it would seem that a terrible injustice is involved in forgiveness.

When we look at sin and righteousness as a matter of relationships, the fuller truth emerges. For when the Holy Spirit convicts that man of sin, he won't just convict him of the sin of adultery; he will convict him of the sin of violating relationships. The Holy Spirit will break that man's heart about his own selfishness, insensitivity, foolishness, and irresponsibility. It won't be a matter of his just standing up one day and saying, "I broke the law of God, but Jesus died to forgive me of all my violations, so everything is cool; I'm forgiven." It will be a matter of coming to God (and to his own wife) and saying, "My heart is broken because of what I've done; I throw myself on your mercy. Please forgive me." Under such circumstances, God's grace flows, and relationships can begin to be renewed.

Let me repeat: The Holy Spirit is not so interested in our living up to external standards as he is in our living in right relationship with God and with each other. True righteousness will focus us on God's values—and his most valuable treasure is people.

A year ago a pastor friend of mine spent some time in Guatemala. While he was there, he was discussing with one of the political leaders of that country why the mission work from America was not having much effect on his country.

"Do you know your neighbors?" the Guatemalan politician asked.

My pastor friend responded sadly, "No, not very well."

"How long have you lived in your present location?" he was asked.

"A couple of years."

Then the leader said this. "I've been in America, and I've watched what is going on there for the last twenty years. When you knew your neighbors well enough to ask to borrow a cup of sugar from them, drugs were not a major problem; neither was crime your greatest fear. The Christianity you had then was worth exporting. But today you have lost the value of relationships. That loss has not only destroyed your society; it has diluted your gospel."

Maybe this political leader knew more about the essence of righteousness than many of the religious leaders guiding the church.

When Paul said he wanted to have a kind of righteousness that comes by faith, he was talking about a righteousness that makes men and women right in their relationship with God and with each other. That kind of righteousness will produce true holy living, not just an external appearance of goodness. It will produce an inner confidence, not self-righteousness.

Jesus fulfilled the law. That's why it is not necessary for you to spend your time stewing about all the legal rights and wrongs and whether you are managing to attain righteousness and avoid sin. Instead, focus on Christ and your relationship with him. Be willing to give that relationship top priority in your life. Make the choice to put your past behind you and press forward toward the life he wants to give you.

HOW TO LIVE BY THE SPIRIT

In the past four chapters we have been exploring the characteristics of the life of the Spirit that displaces the life of the flesh. But living in the Spirit is always a choice. It is the choice to embrace the reality of God's values, to focus on his life. And that is a positive choice. It's none of this "deny the flesh in order to live by the Spirit," but rather "walk by the Spirit and you will not carry out the desire of the flesh" (Gal 5:16). And in Philippians 3, Paul not only outlines the key difference between flesh and Spirit; he also gives his own strategy for learning to "live by the Spirit."

Paul knew that he had lived many years controlled by the old program, the flesh. He knew that he was constantly in a battle with that old programming and that a choice had to be made to set his mind on the things of the Spirit, not on the things of the flesh. And so, out of his own struggle, he gives us a series of clues about to how faith can operate in the process of learning to live by the Spirit:

> I count all things to be loss in view of the surpassing value of knowing Christ Jesus my Lord.... that I may know him and the power of his resurrection and the fellowship of his sufferings, being conformed to his death; in order that I may attain to the resurrection from the dead. Not that I have already obtained it, or have already become perfect, but I press on in order that I may lay hold of that for which also I was laid hold of by Christ Jesus. Brethren, I do not regard myself as having laid hold of it yet; but one thing I do: forgetting what lies behind and reaching forward to what lies ahead, I press on toward the goal for the prize of the upward call of God in Christ Jesus. **Phil 3:8-14**

What guidelines can we find for our own lives in Paul's description of how to live by the Spirit?

1. First, count every asset as a loss. It was as if Paul was sitting there with a ledger and marking everything he considered an asset—his knowledge, his position, his heritage—as a loss. Everything that was a negative he counted on the positive side, realizing that God works through weaknesses to express his glory. The God who creates something out of nothing is a God who will express his glory through the nothingness of our lives.

2. Second, count everything a loss in comparison to knowing Christ. To know Christ, to be found in him, and to have an understanding of a "by faith" righteousness were the highest goals in Paul's life. Everything was to be measured in comparison to this highest value.

3. Third, take all the life of Christ. Paul essentially said, "I have chosen to receive all of his life—not just his power and his perfection, but also his suffering, his rejection. I even choose to receive his death so that I might also have his resurrection."

Some of us, in accepting Christ, still try to pick and choose the best aspects of his life. It's as if we wouldn't mind being the miracle worker or the teacher, but we don't want to suffer, to be misjudged and rejected unjustly. We certainly don't want to die. Yet Paul said, "I want to embrace, receive, identify with every aspect of Jesus' life so that I can attain all that he wants for me."

4. Fourth, set your face toward God's purpose for you. Paul realized that he was still in process, that he had not yet attained his goal. He still had to battle the flesh mentality, but he had set his face toward that which God had in mind when he called him. In other words, he consciously gave up any other ambitions, desires, and plans contrary to God's perfect plan for his life.

5. And fifth, put the past behind you. Paul said that he pressed toward the goal, "forgetting what lies behind." Forget the good and the bad. Forget all the accomplishments and the failures. Live today with the knowledge that you are righteous through faith in Christ Jesus.

Now, putting the past behind you does not mean denying the past. It may well mean making the effort to face your past—to acknowledge your past pain, to forgive others and ask forgiveness, to ask God's help in letting go. But all this must be done in the interest of moving on, "reaching forward to what lies ahead." For the life in Christ that lies ahead of us—"the upward call of God in Jesus Christ"—truly a prize that makes the struggle worthwhile.

CHAPTER 10 Disappointed Expectations

GLORIA SAT VERY STILL, listening as the youth leader exhorted his audience of young people: "Everyone who asks receives... and to [everyone] who knocks it shall be opened" (Mt 7:8). Gloria was attending the meeting with a friend. She had never taken this "Christian life thing" very seriously; however, Gloria was very worried about her parents' impending divorce, and the "ask and knock" idea sounded pretty good.

"I think I'll try it," she decided. "I'm going to ask God to keep Mom and Dad from splitting up. I'll do everything this guy is saying. I'll ask in Jesus' name and I'll ask in faith."

As the days and weeks passed, Gloria constantly reminded herself that she had followed the youth leader's specific instructions about prayer, so surely God would prevent the pain of her family's breakup.

Both her mom and dad tried to prepare her for the impending divorce. They shared their intentions and the reasons for the divorce, but Gloria wouldn't listen. She had prayed. She had faith.

When her parents emerged from the courtroom with the final divorce decree, Gloria was devastated. God had failed her! Now she felt like a fool for ever believing in the first place. "I'll never fall for that stuff again," she vowed. "It doesn't work."

Twelve years later, Gloria's husband, Ben, suggested they should "start taking the kids to church."

"Go ahead if you believe that stuff," Gloria replied, "but I won't be a part of the charade. I know firsthand that faith just doesn't get you anywhere."

Gloria's skepticism is the result of disappointed expectations. She had expected something of God, and God had not responded the way she thought he should. As a result, she was convinced that God had let her down.

In a way, that was the Pharisees' problem, too. They could not accept Jesus because he didn't live up to their expectations. They had created their own concept of what God's promised kingdom would be like. And the idea that God's kingdom could come through a lowly Nazarene seemed foreign and foolish to them.

All of us know what it is like to be disappointed by unrealized expectations. Too many people are living today with dashed hopes and unfulfilled dreams. Disappointment and disillusionment are major problems not only among the unchurched, but even among God's people. We all need a clear word for those times when our expectations are unrealized—and especially when we feel that God has let us down.

OUR EXPECTATIONS VERSUS GOD'S PLAN

The first step in dealing with disappointment and disillusionment is to clarify what our expectations were in the first place. Usually, when our expectations have not been met, we find that our expectations were not based on reality in the first place. Putting our confidence on unrealistic or impossible expectations will always set us up for disappointment.

This is especially true of our expectations for what God will do in our lives. Often, for example, we feel that God has let us down because we have confused human expectations with biblical faith. We put the label "faith" on our human hopes and dreams rather than on God's nature and his promises to us—and then we get bent out of shape when those hopes and dreams don't work out. We fall into the trap of telling God what to do. Then we don't even recognize God's faithfulness because we have our own preconceived notions about how God should work.

Why didn't things turn out according to Gloria's specific request? We can only speculate about Gloria's motives and faith, but we know God did not break his promise. His faithfulness to Gloria simply did not take the form she expected. She was trusting that an event would be changed rather than trusting a Person to be her strength and guide.

Is it wrong to pray specifically, then? No! Biblical faith prays for specific concerns and makes specific requests, but it leaves the results to God because it trusts in God's character. It doesn't nurse preconceived notions of how God must act.

Look at Jesus' prayer in the Garden of Gethsemane: "Abba! Father! All things are possible for thee; remove this cup from me; yet not what I will, but what thou wilt" (Mk 14:36). This prayer is a model of biblical faith. It does contain a very specific personal request—to be spared the crucifixion. But it precedes that request with a confession of faith in God's ability. And it concludes with a statement of personal faith in God's goodness and wisdom. Jesus was not praying out of human expectations, but out of deep trust in God's character and love. And as a result, he yielded to God's plan rather than being disappointed that God was not doing things his way.

When I was a freshman in college, I learned firsthand that God's plans and my expectations aren't always the same thing. As a high school senior, I had yielded my life to Christian ministry and chosen to attend a private denominational university to prepare for my life's vocation. I had also received a football scholarship. My prayer was constantly, "Lord, help me to be a good football player, and I will use that athlete's platform to speak for you."

I honestly thought God and I had a deal. He would help me

be a successful athlete, and I in turn would help him reach football-smitten youngsters with the gospel.

I was on the starting team most of my freshman year and showed great promise. Then, in the last game of the season, I was blocked from behind and suffered a fractured hip. After lying immobile in the hospital for several weeks, I was told by my doctor that I would never play football again.

I was devastated! "I can't keep my promise to God. What good will I be to him now? No one will want to hear my story. What kind of hero is a crippled freshman?" I visualized kids' staying away from my speaking engagements in large numbers, mumbling, "Dudley who?"

I thought God wanted a football hero to put in a good word for the gospel. But he just wanted to love *me*. I shall never forget that day alone in hospital room number 101 when I admitted, "Oh, God, I can't do anything you wanted me to do!" And I heard God reply, "I love you just like you are. I don't want a hero. I just want you." My human expectations were replaced by a broader and deeper understanding of God's call and promise to me. He can be trusted.

ONLY GOD CAN PRODUCE WHAT GOD PROMISES

We will inevitably be disappointed whenever we substitute human expectations for that wonderful eternal quality of faith. What is faith? It is that quiet confidence in God's character that releases me to act on a specific word of God given to me.

Biblical faith is that wonderful God-given ability to see the invisible, then operate according to the reality of that invisible world. True biblical faith is closely connected with hope; Hebrews 11:1 explains that "faith is the assurance of things hoped for, the conviction of things not seen." Faith always involves patience; there is no faith apart from patience and no patience apart from faith.

Biblical faith is *not* idle hope and wishful thinking. Instead, it is basing our expectations on the Reality at the center of the universe. We can always count on God to keep his promises. When our expectations are based on God's character and his love, they will never be disappointed. I've discovered that when I act according to biblical faith, I have the great privilege of seeing God at work and cooperating with him in his redemptive plan.

Human expectations, on the other hand, grow out of human needs and human imagination and fallen human nature, not the mind of God. Often these human visions grow out of the desire to have our needs met or to get our own way. They may also arise from the desire to make a splash in the world, to be significant by accomplishing something on our own. Because they are based in our finite human nature rather than in the eternal and faithful God, in the long run all our human expectations are doomed to disappointment.

In addition, of course, these mind-induced visions invariably leave us feeling responsible to help make the vision happen. But biblical faith views the invisible with the realization that only God can produce what God promises.

The greatest illustration of this would be Abraham and Sarah. God had promised them descendants. However, when the promised children didn't materialize, they began to feel they had to help God accomplish his promise to them. Sarah sent Abraham a child by her maid—and the result was nothing but heartbreak and household strife. If we could only understand the eternal truth that only God can produce what God promises, what freedom we would have from trying to live up to our own faulty expectations.

GOD'S WAY IS ALWAYS BIGGER AND BETTER

What happens when we humans step in to try to fulfill our own vision—either of what we want or of what God wants?

One result is burnout and guilt. We often feel disappointed

because we don't understand what God expects of us. Many people wear themselves out with activities that have nothing to do with God's expectations of them. He simply expects us to trust him. There is nothing that pleases him more than for us to live in dependence on him as we become an expression of his life on the earth. To trust him and thus become faithful stewards of his resources is the sum total of God's expectations for us. Yet so many of us live under a false sense of guilt because we feel we are not living up to what we perceive as God's expectation for our lives.

But there's another result of living by our own expectations. The human mind will limit the manifestation only to its visualized result, so we always end up underestimating what God wants to accomplish. Inevitably, we undershoot—and the result is disillusionment.

We should get some clue as to our limited expectation from statements in Scripture such as, "Now to him who is able to do exceeding abundantly beyond all that we ask or think" (Eph 3:20). When God works, what he is doing will always be beyond our ability to visualize. A God-given vision requires God-given understanding.

So don't misunderstand. God is not seeking to steal your visions from you. He doesn't want you to live without expectations. He wants you to base your expectations on his character and his promises. He's trying to give you a vision that is beyond anything your human mind can create.

The results of God's speaking to us will always be more than and different from what the human mind can conceive. If we too closely tie human expectations to God's visions, we will miss what God is saying, because it won't look like our human visualization.

The kingdom of heaven is a realm greater than the kingdoms of this earth. When we are born again, we can truly see and embrace the kingdom of heaven. It is a reality. The blessings of that kingdom can be enjoyed regardless of what is going on in the physical realm. In fact, embracing this invisible kingdom affects the visible world positively.

The Pharisees were right. God *had* promised that he was going to establish a kingdom on the earth. For hundreds of years the covenant people looked forward to that kingdom. They would have testified that they were living by faith, and yet they reduced God's promise to a human visualization of how it would be. Then, when Jesus came and announced the kingdom was here, none of them could recognize it. The fulfillment of God's promise was totally different from the human expectation of that promise.

Is it possible that some of the disappointments you feel at times in your own life come from painting too small a picture of what God had promised you when, in reality, what he is doing in your life is bigger than and different from what you expected?

You can be sure of one thing. God's promises to you *will* come to pass. He has reserved the liberty and love of Jesus' life for you as you trust his Word to you. Remember, there were four hundred years between the Old Testament and the New Testament. Many generations of people were told that one day God's promised king would reign and that his kingdom would bless the earth. I'm sure it seemed to many of them that it would never come to pass.

Then one day, in a way that the human mind would have never imagined, a strange-looking man stood on the banks of the Jordan River and lifted his voice to all who would hear: "Repent, for the kingdom of heaven is at hand." In a very short time he introduced the Lamb of God who would take away the sin of the world—by dying and rising from the dead! God had kept his promise... but it didn't look like anything mere human minds had visualized.

DISAPPOINTED IN EACH OTHER

Not all our disappointed expectations arise from disappointment with God, of course. In all our relationships we find conflicts rising from unrealized expectations. When others expect me to do what I never intend to do, I will always be a failure in their eyes. Therefore, it becomes necessary that I clarify what is expected of me in every relationship.

In my itinerant ministry, I have been asked hundreds of times to come and minister in different churches. When I first began receiving requests, my response was, "If they want me and I have the date available, I'll come." However, I soon found myself in some situations where my abilities and the churches' desires didn't match. Some wanted me to attract the youth. Some wanted city-wide evangelistic crusades. Others wanted me to teach the people to give so the church could meet the budget.

So after awhile I learned to ask a simple question before accepting a request to speak: "What are you expecting of me?" This way we clarify our expectations from the beginning. I am not pushed to misuse my gifts, and they are not disappointed. I want to know if I can produce what they expect (realizing that I by myself produce nothing, but God through his gifts accomplishes his works through me).

It's vital to remember: I can be doing my best and still fail in your eyes if you are expecting results I cannot produce.

Have you ever had the fascinating experience of discussing with your mate how different marriage is from what you expected it to be? Almost all of us married people face the problem of disappointed expectations at some point in our lives together.

My wife knew before we were married that I was a country boy and that, like most country boys, I was used to getting up early. My dad felt like it was a good idea to get a good start on the day by getting up early in the morning. During much of my early life, I usually got up between four-thirty and five o'clock in the morning. So when we married, Betsy naturally assumed that, consistent with my upbringing, I'd be an early riser.

What Betsy didn't realize was that during all those years I had hated getting up early! I would much rather have rescheduled the days to begin about nine in the morning and end at two o'clock the following morning.

For the first few months of our marriage, Betsy thought I was sick because I didn't rise cheerfully at five o'clock. Later she began to be irritated. She wanted to get up early and fix a big southern breakfast of eggs, bacon, and biscuits with homemade fig preserves. Unfortunately, I just couldn't face scrambled eggs that early in the morning. I would sit sleepily at the breakfast table staring at those eggs. She thought I didn't like her cooking.

On the other hand, I liked to stay up late. In my opinion, midnight was a good time to think deeply and engage in meaningful conversation. But after rising at five o'clock in the morning to prepare a big breakfast, Betsy couldn't keep her eyes open. "Is she not interested in me? Have I already lost my romantic appeal? This girl won't stay awake to be with me."

Even though we had dated for four years, Betsy and I didn't really know what to expect from each other. These and other differences have emerged as our relationship has grown. Many expectations have had to be laid down in order to discover reality. These differences can be amusing or irritating, depending on our willingness to adjust our expectations.

I've very much appreciated a relationship with one particular friend who always asks, when he begins to get close to someone, "What can I do for you?" What he means is, "What are you looking for from me?" If the other person is looking for something he can't deliver, he quickly clarifies that point so the relationship can operate more smoothly.

Clarifying expectations is essential to avoid disappointment in relationships. It prevents misunderstandings that come from unspoken and unrecognized agendas. And it paves the way for true accountability as well.

DISAPPOINTED IN THE CHURCH

Do you know anyone who has been disappointed in a relationship with a church? Could it be that one of the reasons for our disillusionment could be found in improper expectations?

For example, some people look to a church to solve their problems. But as far as I can tell, from my reading of Scripture and my personal experience, God wants us to work through our own problems in dependence on him, discovering Jesus to be the source of everything we need and other relationships to be his channels.

While on the earth, Jesus was a little put out with those who wanted their needs met but were unwilling to buy the whole "kingdom package" of love, honesty, ministry, and service. Those who followed him only for the bread he could multiply turned away when he invited them to eat his body and drink his blood (Jn 6:26-66).

Particularly in Western culture, too many of us have begun to look at the church in the same way we view the federal government—as a big brother, existing to meet our needs as we perceive them according to our agenda—and we judge the church according to its success in doing that. If that has been your approach the church will fail, because the church was not designed by God to be a substitute for your relationship with him and with others.

Some have been offended and disappointed in church leadership. One of the reasons is that Christian leaders have feet of clay and have failed on many occasions. Another reason is that we have faulty expectations for the role Christian leaders should play in our lives.

I know many church members, for example, who become disillusioned with their pastor because they expect the pastor to be a spiritual caretaker to them. But that's not the role the Bible assigns to pastors!

The New Testament uses the word *pastor* primarily as a verb —and it applies to all Christians. All of us are called to "shepherd" others—to help sheep to grow and mature. We can feed them, help guide them, and protect them. That's the work of all the saints.

So what's the role of the pastor? The primary use of *pastor* as a noun in the New Testament is in Ephesians 4:11, where

Paul mentions "pastors" as one of leaders God gives the church. Then, in the same passage, Paul outlines the proper expectation for these leaders: *equipping the saints for the work of the ministry.*

The pastor is not the chief executive officer of the church. The pastor is not the janitor in charge of cleaning up all the messes. The pastor is not even the one who does all the hands-on ministry. The pastor's job (along with the apostles, prophets, evangelists, and teachers) is to equip church members to "pastor" others!

Jesus, by his own example, even shows pastors how to carry out this equipping. It goes like this:

Phase 1 Take them with you and let them watch you.
Phase 2 Then send them out and watch them, encouraging, advising, and teaching.
Phase 3 Finally, send them out with your blessing, your presence, and your commitment always to be there for support.

Those three phases, in a nutshell, summarize God's expectations for a pastor. If you're looking to your pastor for something different than that, you have an improper expectation. Your pastor will fail in your eyes, because God will not help someone do that which is contrary to what God has assigned that person to do.

RESISTING FALSE EXPECTATIONS

When Jesus came to the earth, he refused to live according to the expectations of others. He refused to live up to others' concept of what a Messiah should be. Many expected him to heal all the sick, raise all the dead, fix all the problems. He quickly revealed that he would not be pushed into that role, and he illustrated that fact in his relationship with his best friend, Lazarus. When Lazarus was sick, Jesus would not even go to his bedside; in fact, he waited until his friend had died.

He had faced the same issue earlier when Satan tempted him in the wilderness. Satan had been trying to get Jesus to operate out of preconceived notions of what the Messiah would do: "If you are the Messiah, throw yourself from the pinnacle of the temple and people will believe" (Mt 4:1-11, paraphrased).

If Jesus had fallen into the trap of trying to meet the misguided expectations of those around him, the glory of God's ultimate plan would not have been revealed through him. Lazarus was not just healed, but raised from the dead. And by refusing to reveal his person in an improper manner at the improper time in the wilderness, he yielded himself to the fulfillment of God's perfect plan for our redemption.

FAITH WILL NOT DISAPPOINT

Expectations are wonderful, but faith vision is even better, for it gives God the opportunity to be himself without having to live up to our limited perspectives and misapplied expectations. If given the chance, God will fulfill his Word to you, and the results will be greater than and different from anything your human mind could ever conceive. His work will satisfy your every need, and you will find yourself worshiping him.

There is a sense in which we must wait for the intervention of God. But even in those waiting times we must remember that God has *already* intervened. Jesus has already come. The Holy Spirit has already been given. Divine life has already been imparted. God is to be experienced *now.* We cannot make him do anything before his time, but he is doing more now than any of us can conceive.

Real faith does not impose itself on other people. It doesn't coerce others to do that which is contrary to their choice. God's kind of faith allows us to enjoy the fullness of God's personality now and to operate according to his calendar as he fulfills his promises.

I encourage you that if you are living with some degree of disappointment or disillusion because of unfulfilled expectations concerning your relationship with the church, a spiritual leader, a mate, a friend, or whomever, remember the Word of God promises that "hope in the glory of God... does not disappoint" (Rom 5:2, 5). Biblical faith that is based on the character of God will not disappoint. He cannot do anything bad in your life, regardless of how it may appear right now, because he himself is nothing but good. And he is doing good in your circumstances. As a result, you can have peace in your heart and joy in your spirit.

CHAPTER

11 Religion or Relationship?

ARE YOU TIRED OF THE PHARISEES YET? I hope so. I hope you get so tired of "substitute life" that you discard it forever and embrace the reality of God's abundant life offered in Jesus. At the risk of being redundant, however, I want to linger with the Pharisees just long enough to examine some of the practical aspects of the legalistic mentality.

But first a review question: How can you recognize a Pharisee—or recognize the elements of Pharisaism in yourself? We have explored some of the facets: blindness to spiritual reality, emphasis on sacrifice rather than mercy, focus on the flesh, a confusion of human expectations for biblical faith. But here are the two characteristics that unmistakably mark a Pharisee:

1. Pharisees invariably focus on the external and ignore the internal. Pharisees are religious people who have not registered the message of the new covenant: "I will put my laws into their minds, and I will write them upon their hearts" (Heb 8:10). They seem oblivious to a lifestyle of holiness that comes from within. The result is a shallow religionist who works on the outside without first addressing the inner person—a hypocrite who does some proper activities but out of impure motives.

2. Pharisees Always Display a Dominant Religious Spirit. Some Bible interpreters believe that the devil was a worship leader in heaven before he was cast out because of his rebellion. Therefore, the devil by nature is religious and everything he touches has religious flavor to it.

Whether or not that's true, human beings are created in God's image and, even in our fallen state, we are inherently religious. It should be no surprise to us, then, that the perverted and counterfeit forms of life will always have religion associated with them. The strongest of the strongholds in the demonic realm are those where religious spirits are entrenched. Religious words, activities, and rituals have been used throughout the centuries to cover human insecurity, greed, lust, and selfish ambition. Granted, it is a thin disguise. But it has been used successfully throughout the years, and continues to be used today.

Jesus directly addressed these issues of holy hypocrisy and perverted religion in his famous Sermon on the Mount (Mt 5-7). He used three illustrations: prayer, fasting, and giving. And what he had to say about these three "religious" practices still gives us practical perspectives on them today.

"WHEN YOU PRAY..."

Jesus chided the Pharisees for their focus on the externals of prayer—reciting long, loud prayers in public in order to command respect. He suggested a simple form of prayer to serve as a model for all Christians (Mt 5:5-13). But despite Jesus' straightforward example, God's people still wrangle over the external issues of prayer: How often should we pray? What are the right words to use? What bodily position must we assume to get things accomplished?

For example, how many books will have to be written before we finally settle the issue of the best time to pray? Some authors suggest that if we don't pray early in the morning we are not giving God the first fruits of the day. Some say that once a day is not enough, that if the Moslems can pray several times a day facing toward their Mecca, the Christian should pray at least three times daily... morning, noon, and night. Some others have suggested that since the number seven is the number of completeness, a person has not prayed sufficiently unless he has prayed distinctly seven times a day.

The position of prayer also seems to be a matter of great concern. Should we pray on our knees? Should we pray with our heads down in humility, recognizing that we are only humans in the presence of God? Or should we, with the recognition that we have been redeemed, always pray with upturned faces?

What words should we use to begin our prayers? Does "Dear God" suffice? Should we mention the Father, the Son, or the Holy Spirit? Does God answer prayer that is addressed to the wrong person of the Trinity?

One morning our Friday businessmen's Bible study included a man who had just come to know Jesus as his personal Savior the previous weekend. Before the Bible study started, he raised his hand: "Could I ask a question about prayer?" he said. I thought he was going to get into some deep theological question about how God answers prayer or how he could get the most out of his prayer life. But his refreshing, innocent question was, "What do I call God when I start praying? Do I say 'Mr.' or 'dear' or 'sir'?"

I was rebuked by the simplicity of that question. My mind had already run off into some complicated explanations about how prayer and faith work. But that man really put his finger on the basic issue, which is: "How do we relate to God in prayer?"

Could we just agree on the simple essence of prayer? It is relationship, not religion. In fact, prayer is open communion with God himself. It is made possible by the shed blood of Jesus, who gives us free and continual access to the presence of God. We pray to God "in Jesus' name" not because we need to invoke a formula, but because only Jesus has a right to talk to the Father face to face. We can speak to God because that right has been granted to us through Jesus' death, burial, and resurrection. In fact, one reason God the Father likes for us to pray is that our prayer shows great appreciation for the payment he made through his Son on the cross.

There is no reason for any of us to live in loneliness or isolation. God the Father is always available to talk to his children. He has not only invited us in to pray, he has commanded us to come in to pray. The externals of prayer are not the issue. Fellowship is the issue.

The question of fellowship informs the question of "how often," too. Through the years I've had several young ministers come to me and begin quizzing me on my prayer life. They want to know, for instance, what time I get up in the morning to pray, how long I pray, what I pray for, and how the discipline of prayer has affected my life.

One time a young man asked, "How many minutes a day would you say you spend praying?" In an effort to shock him away from the externals, I replied, "Take your choice. All day or not at all."

My point was that communion with God is not limited to the times a person is verbally voicing a prayer. I would honestly have to say that most of my prayers start off with the word *and*: "... and Father, how should I respond to that remark?" I am not promoting irreverence; I'm just exercising a privilege obtained for me through the shed blood of Jesus Christ. Because Christ has redeemed me, I can approach God freely as my Father, depending upon the Holy Spirit to interpret to God my desires and to interpret to me God's desires. All during the day, God and I talk about the events of the day and the circumstances surrounding us. I may ask many questions throughout the day, and I say "thank you" often as I watch his bountiful blessings unfold.

I'm obviously not saying we shouldn't set aside time for undistracted fellowship with the Father. I'm simply stressing that prayer should not be governed by externals. In its essence, it is communion with God, and it can happen at any time, in any position, in any words. I have even discovered that God is able to speak to us in our sleep—that even sleep does not interrupt the openness of heaven for those who desire fellowship with the Father.

WHENEVER YOU FAST...

Jesus also addressed the practice of fasting, which the Pharisees used as a way to draw attention to their pious spirituality (Mt 6:16-17). They would pour ashes on themselves, tear their clothes, and make it very obvious to everyone that they were involved in an act of self-sacrifice. Clearly they were saying to all around, "Look at what we're doing for God!"

This kind of attitude toward fasting originates partly in the assumption that we can "pay for gain with pain." There's a phrase often heard on the lips of the religious: "We must pay the price." That in a sense is true; suffering does come to those who follow Christ. However, we must always remember that the primary price has already been paid. Jesus paid the price for all the blessings that God gives to us; we are, in fact, joint heirs with Jesus. He has paid the price by his death, and we can freely reap the benefits.

Remember it is mercy, not sacrifice, that pleases God. God is never wooed into doing our bidding because of the price we pay in any self-contrived sacrifice, including fasting. Sacrifice done for the purpose of drawing attention to ourselves really misses the point.

I have noticed in my own experience that it is very difficult not to mention to others my deeds of sacrifice. For instance, when I have fasted for several days, it is so easy to let it become a part of my conversation: "The other day while I was fasting God spoke to me..." Now this could be a very accurate statement—but often my real purpose in mentioning it is to let others know what I am doing.

Jesus clearly skewered that motivation in the Pharisees: "Beware of practicing your righteousness before men to be noticed by them; otherwise you have no reward with your Father who is in heaven" (Mt 6:1). And the fact is, the Pharisees did *all* of their religious acts to be seen by others, for they were preoccupied with the external.

Is fasting valid? Sure it is. Jesus didn't say *if* you fast, but *when* you fast. But his emphasis on fasting was the internal, not the external. In fact, he told his followers to fast in secret. "Wash your face," he says. Forego the ashes. Resist the temptation to let everyone know what you're doing. Instead, concentrate on drawing close to God.

Jesus reminds us that fasting is for our benefit, not God's. We as Christians have the wonderful privilege of living in two worlds at the same time. We are spiritual beings living in a physical body. Sometimes the external world of the physical becomes so consuming that the spirit withers. When we fast, we make a conscious choice to de-emphasize the physical in order to give the spiritual a chance to be renewed and released. The result is a heightened awareness of the spiritual world, a more clearly defined faith, and a higher level of spiritual energy. That's a far better "payoff" than just being recognized by others for our sacrifice!

WHEN YOU GIVE...

Jesus also had some straightforward things to say about the issue of giving (Mt 6:1-4). The Pharisees would give alms in order to be honored by other people. They would have a trumpet sounded before them in the streets as they made their way to the temple to contribute.

Religious giving has been used in many unscrupulous ways throughout history. Some, for instance, have tried to use God and his kingdom as a kind of "holy stock market" to gain personal wealth. They've taken God-given principles such as

"Give and it will be given back to you" and "You sow what you reap"—and used them in the service of greed.

But the fact that God's principles of giving have been abused does not make them less valid!

Regardless of the "holy investment" abusers, for instance, it is true that whatever we give to God he gives back to us. First of all, he does not need it. Second, giving is part of his design by which we can maintain a proper perspective of who we are and why we are put on earth. He is the owner, we are the managers. Those who still believe they are the owners of their physical possessions have not even made the first step in learning to be managers of God's possessions.

It is also true that we sow what we reap. (See Galatians 6:7.) We plant the seed, and we can be assured that the seed will come up, kind for kind. If we plant corn, we will harvest corn. If we plant anger and bitterness, we will reap a bitter harvest. God has established that we human beings reap what we sow. It is an established fact that more will come up than was planted (Lk 6:38). That also is by God's design—the law of the harvest. If it weren't a fact, there would be no need for the planting in the first place.

These basic principles hold. They are God's, not ours, even when we try to exploit them for our benefit.

Note this fact: Our Father God likes being God. He has built into his "sow and reap" principles a few angles that remind us that he is in charge and will not be used for our own greedy gain.

For one thing, God has given us the responsibility for sowing and reaping, but he has left the seasons in his own hands. There is a time of waiting between planting and the harvest, and it cannot be manipulated by human beings. The seed *will* come up sooner or later. It will be later than the planting, but how much later is left to God alone.

Another way God controls the harvest is through drought. I remember talking to some peanut farmers in South Alabama a couple of years ago. These farmers had spent thousands of dollars planting their crops, expecting a bountiful harvest, but drought had come, and nobody was harvesting peanuts. The drought had made a statement about the limits of human control.

Generally, what we reap depends on what we sow; productivity is in direct proportion to the investment. But drought can change all that. There will be times when, regardless of what we have sown, we don't harvest anything. It's as if God is saying to us that he wants us to trust him *as a person*, not just his principles. Those who try to use the principles of giving to manipulate God and his kingdom will find themselves broken by sovereignly planned droughts and delayed harvest.

There is obviously more to the question of giving than the "reap and sow" question. God has also commanded us to give, and that raises its own set of questions. I'm sure if you've been around church activities for very long, you've heard people discuss the tithe. All kinds of questions are asked about the tithe. For instance, should we tithe on the gross or on the net? (The cute answer is, "Do you want to be blessed on the gross or the net?") Is the tithe one-tenth, or one-third, or what?

But here again, the issue is that of external appearance versus spiritual reality. As long as we are focused on the externals, giving will become at best a chore, at worst a manipulative tool to gain attention for ourselves or to get God to bless us according to our agenda. When we focus on internal, spiritual reality, giving becomes the first grade in God's school of management.

Remember, God put human beings on the earth to manage the earth. We who have been redeemed from the Fall by the death of Jesus Christ have been given the opportunity to manage under God's direction.

There's more. Jesus said that if we are faithful in little things, we will be given responsibility for much. To most humans, money is the most important thing we have. To God, it is of little value except as the first test of stewardship. Those who fail that test do not get an opportunity to take any others. (See Luke 16:10-12.)

Seen in this light, stewardship becomes not just a matter of how much we give, but of how we handle all our possessions. How much we spend, how much we save, or how much we invest are just as important as how much we give. All these activities are part of our job as managers in God's kingdom. God's concept of appropriate giving reaches far beyond the tithe.

But you may be protesting, "I've been tithing exactly ten percent since I was a little child; are you saying I was wrong?" Of course not. I'm sure you've been blessed in your giving, for God has blessed your obedience to the level of light that you have received. But now God is inviting you to adopt a broader perspective of your assignment as a manager. He wants you to give not only because it is something you *ought* to do, but because it is something you *want* to do, and because you're learning how to handle his resources under his direction.

Those who internalize the gospel never do less than those who externalize it. Those who are motivated by love will always do more than those seeking to perform in order to be accepted— and they will do it with much joy and great peace.

DO I NEED TO GO TO CHURCH?

Though Jesus does not address the issue of church attendance in this passage of the Sermon on the Mount, it is closely related in principle to the issues of prayer, fasting, and giving. Jesus did speak to the Pharisees about wanting the prominent seats in the synagogue when they attended. (See Matthew 23:1-7.) Again, this reveals the Pharisees' total misunderstanding of God's purposes. Because their focus was so external and their insecurities so great, their primary motive in seeking a prominent position "at church" was to appear righteous before other people.

To you who attend church because you "should"—to fend off evil for the rest of the week, to give yourself a good reputation in the community, or to give your children the idea that you are an upstanding person—let me suggest that there's a better way. You can, in fact, *enjoy* fellowship with the body of Christ.

Overall church attendance has dropped in recent years because so many people have been bored with the experience. But boredom doesn't have to be the order to the day. In fact, I will give you a "money back" guarantee that when you see the church for what it really is, church attendance will no longer be boring. It will become as essential in your life as food and drink.

God has designed us as depositories of his life, but he has not given all of it to any one of us. In order to be complete, we must relate to the rest of the body. There are things that other members of the body can do for me that I cannot do for myself. This does not mean that I am ever to become totally dependent upon other Christians. But it does mean that, in my dependence upon God, I am interdependent upon those in the body who are gifted differently than I.

Those of us who have grown up in a free culture tend to undervalue the privilege of just being with other saints. Instead of treasuring the gifts and the differences of our fellow members of Christ's body, we put all our hope in the event of the worship service. In fact, we often come expecting to be entertained. If the church service does not "do something" for us, we judge it a failure.

But in those parts of the world where the issue is life and not performance, Christians will sacrifice their lives in an effort just to be with one another. They have realized that in each other's presence they experience a release of energy greater than they can ever experience alone. They also realize that God did not design us for isolation and loneliness. His design was for fellowship, not only with him but with each other.

"Let us hold fast the confession of our hope... not forsaking our own assembling together, as is the habit of some" (Heb

10:23-25). This is not a command from God telling us that we had better attend church every Sunday for fear that if we don't our business will fail or we will get sick. It's an exhortation from our loving Father not to allow anything to keep us from the channel of blessing he has designed for us.

FREE FROM THE PHARISEE IN ME

A preoccupation with the external and an obsession with the religious define the Pharisaical mindset—and we are all vulnerable to thinking this way. But when we embrace the essence of the life of Jesus, we are set free from "the Pharisee in me."

What is life like once we've stopped thinking like Pharisees? We find ourselves being supernaturally natural. We can be real without fear of being wrong. Our motivation comes out of the inner person where the law of God has been written. Lifeless religion leaves a bad taste in our mouth. We refuse to categorize our lives into secular and spiritual, because we have found that the glory of God fills the whole earth and the whole earth belongs to him. The essence of our religion is not external performance but internal relationship.

There's more. If we have experienced the joy of God's unconditional love, we will want to express that love to the needy around us. As a general rule, we become people who are fun to be with—neither judgmental nor self-conscious. We are able to listen to anyone's perspective, believing that difference is good and not evil. We resist the temptation of trying to conform everyone to our own image, and we dare to believe that righteousness is stronger than wickedness. As a result, we enjoy the confidence to enter into any realm of life without fear.

If the life I've just described feels familiar, great! But if you have just recognized some Pharisee in you, it's time for a reality check. Honesty is the key to breaking free from Pharisaism.

To acknowledge darkness in your life is to expose it to the very light of God. When his light is allowed to flow into your life, darkness will dissipate. Relationship with him is much better than any religious form. If you have found yourself thinking at any time, "Thank you, God, that I'm not like some of these sinners," then I would suggest you pray this prayer: "Have mercy upon me, a sinner." (See Luke 18:11-13.)

And the good news to all us Pharisees is: "His loving kindness is everlasting" (Ps 100:5).

PART THREE

Grace and the Life of Liberty

It was for freedom that Christ set us free; therefore keep standing firm and do not be subject again to a yoke of slavery. **Galatians 5:1**

CHAPTER 12

And *That's* the Gospel!

OL' JOHN, THE SMALL-TOWN barbershop philosopher, was expanding his homespun philosophy about the superiority of the dem'crats over the r'publicans. He finished with an exclamation to underscore his veracity: "And that's the gospel!"

Now, we all know John wasn't preaching the gospel. He used that phrase to add credibility to his story. But the word *gospel* really should be more than a byword to verify that someone is telling the truth.

I like the translation of the word *gospel* found in many versions of the Scriptures: "good news." That is exactly what it is. But not just any good news. It is *the* good news about God's attitude toward needy human beings in a fallen world.

Many theories and heresies have been called gospel. To many who grew up hearing the Bible taught, it was not good news at all; instead, it was a restrictive noose around the neck and a heavy weight around the feet. The gospel was presented as something we need to heed in order to make it into heaven, but it certainly was no fun to live with.

The problem, I believe, is that so many proclaimers of the gospel never really have heard it themselves. Consequently, it has become just another ruined word in the vocabulary of fallen human beings as they endeavor to figure out some way to gain favor with God.

THE GOSPEL PLAN

So, what is the *real* gospel? It's the "good news" story of what God has done in his relationship with men and women from the very beginning of time. Here's a "big picture" summary of how it happened:

First of all, remember that God created men and women in his own image, for fellowship with him. But after Adam and Eve sinned in the garden of Eden, society started on a downward spiral toward destruction. With the exception of a few such as Noah, the human race was pretty pitiful. Then God, through his own initiative, found an ordinary man named Abram and made some outlandish promises to him (Gn 12:1-3).

Now, Abram was a polytheist. Until Jehovah appeared to him, Abram had never heard of a single God who could handle all of life's crises. But Abram believed God's promises and thus became Abraham, the "father of faith" (Gal 3:7). God was starting his family of children who would believe him and express his nature throughout eternity.

In order to get people to place their trust in God instead of in themselves, God instituted the law through his servant, Moses. This law not only epitomized the character of God in external form, it also revealed to men and women their inability to live a life righteous enough to please God. The fallen human race was worse off than they realized. They were incapable of living up to the simple commands of God. Thinking they could, they kept on trying—and failing.

Note once more the purpose of the covenant of law. It was never intended to make human beings holy (Gal 2:16); its purpose was to reveal how badly humans need God to act on their behalf. And true to form, humanity misunderstood the ultimate purpose of the old covenant and attempted to use that covenant as a means of attaining righteousness.

But note also the underlying intentions of God. God was never looking for a group of people who could keep a set of rules. He desired a family to share a relationship of love and trust. Over and over he kept reaching out to his people. And the ultimate expression of God's desire for fellowship with the human race came when God decided to take on human flesh himself.

Everything God has ever done was fulfilled in the coming of Jesus. The entire early story of what went on between God and humankind is full of types and shadows that point toward the life, death, and resurrection of Christ. The Psalms and the prophets foretold his coming. The saints of the covenant of law lived in faith, looking for the day that the God of mercy and grace would be revealed in the person of Jesus.

A Tale of Two Covenants. But here's where the story becomes complicated. The coming of Jesus represented a whole new chapter in the covenant relationship between God and humanity. Even after Jesus came, some people insisted on clinging to the types and shadows of the past. They chose the old covenant, with its partial revelation, and rejected the full revelation of grace and truth that came in Jesus.

The apostle Paul, in his letter to the Galatians, draws a beautiful contrast between the two covenants and those that follow them. He uses the allegory of the two women in Abraham's life to demonstrate the difference between the two covenants:

> For it is written that Abraham had two sons, one by the bondwoman [Hagar] and one by the free woman [Sarah]. But the son by the bondwoman [Ishmael] was born according to the flesh, and the son by the free woman [Isaac] through the promise. This is allegorically speaking: for these women are two covenants, one proceeding from Mount Sinai bearing children who are to be slaves; she is Hagar. Now this Hagar... corresponds to the present Jerusalem, for she is in slavery with her children. But the Jerusalem above is free; she is our mother.... And you brethren, like Isaac, are children of promise.... So then, brethren, we are not children of a bondwoman, but of the free woman. **Gal 4:22-31**

In this allegory, Hagar the "bondwoman" clearly represents the old covenant, and Ishmael represents its fruits. Sarah represents the new covenant that is only fulfilled through promise and by faith, and Isaac the fruit of that covenant.

God makes it very clear that the two covenants are not to be mixed: "Cast out the bondwoman and her son" (Gal 4:30). The law covenant was preparation for faith. When faith comes, the old passes away. It was not wrong; it was just replaced by something better.

With this in mind, let's look at some of the obvious contrast between the two covenants.

PRINCIPLES VERSUS PROMISE

First, *the old covenant operated by principles, the new covenant by promise.* The story of Abraham, Sarah, and Hagar clearly illustrates this distinction.

God established the method by which human beings would be born. It is his principle, and it is good. In intimacy, man provides the seed, the woman the egg. Conception subsequently takes place, and something wonderful happens that was conceived in the mind of God alone... a new creature is begun!

The system of human reproduction was God's principle for populating the earth. And this principle works for all tribes and all cultures. It was given to all people, regardless of faith or creed. Even people who do not believe in God operate under this wonderful principle.

With Abraham and Sarah, God waited until this principle was inoperative. He had made the promise while they still had life in their reproductive organs, but he waited to fulfill that promise until they were too old to have children based on the natural principle of reproduction.

Isaac was a product of promise, not just principle. His birth was a miracle of fulfilled promise, not just the natural result of following a principle.

This is not the only time God preempted his principle of human reproduction. Throughout biblical history, we see that many times when God was ready to do something special and new in birthing a human being, he did it through a barren womb. Centuries after the birth of Isaac, at a time when Israel needed a prophet, Samuel came from the barren womb of Hannah. Later, after a four-hundred-year period of silence, God was ready to announce something wonderful to the world, and John the Baptist was born from the barren womb of Elizabeth. And, miracle of miracles, God's climactic birth came from a virgin womb! Jesus was born to the *virgin* Mary.

What does all this mean? God is free to supersede his own laws and cause us to live at a higher level than is feasible to the natural mind. Certainly, nothing is wrong with having babies the natural way. However, God is free to cause reproduction to happen in a supernatural fashion. In so doing, God seeks to raise up a people of faith who are no longer limited by the elemental teachings of the world but who depend instead on God's promises.

This distinction between principles and promise also explains why the apostle Paul chose not to preach anything to the Corinthians other than "Christ, and him crucified" (1 Cor 2:2). That puzzled me somewhat as I thought of all the wonderful Old Testament truths that were readily available to Paul. He could easily have preached Proverbs with all its wisdom. He could have preached Psalms with its varied and creative expressions of intimacy. Or he could have explored the many lessons learned from the history of Israel. Yet he focused completely on his message on Christ crucified. Why? Because Christ's death and resurrection represent the highest and most climactic revelation of God's entire design. It is God's bringing life out of death and something out of nothing according to his promise. That really is *gospel!*

To many, the Christian life is one of discovering the principles that govern each aspect of existence and following them to their conclusion, thus reaping the benefits of adherence to the designer's plan. This is obviously better than neglecting the precepts of God and blindly living with no guide. But there is an even higher form of existence. It is living by faith, developing a vital relationship with God himself and enjoying his presence and personality.

Promises require faith. You can't work a promise. It is not a formula. It can be believed or refused, but it cannot be used as a tool and then set aside until it's needed again. To believe a promise, you must get to know the One who makes the promise. Then you must live in patience and trust and relationship while that promise shapes your life.

STRIVING VERSUS REST

Second, *the old covenant is characterized by striving, the new covenant by rest.* When the pressure is on to perform in order to accomplish the desired objective, strife and labor enter the picture. Can't you just see Abraham and Sarah scheming to find a way to produce a son and coming up with the idea of using Hagar? God had made the promise, but they assumed the responsibility of fulfilling it. They can eternally testify that only God can fulfill the promises he makes. Listen to a possible conversation between Abraham and Sarah:

"Sarah, I don't know what we are going to do. God is expecting us to have a child through which he can bless the world. We are getting old. We've tried everything. What's wrong with us?"

"Well, maybe God expects us to use our imaginations and find a way that is different," replies Sarah. "After all, God is mysterious."

"What do you mean, different?" Abraham queries. "There is only one way to have a child."

"I know, Abraham, but are you aware that the law states that any child born in your house by one of your servants is technically yours?" says Sarah.

"What are you saying, Sarah?"

"Well, Abraham, I guess I'm asking you if you have a better idea?"

So, they found a way to satisfy the law technically and still produce the long-awaited child. There was one major problem. God wouldn't accept their solution, nor would he allow Ishmael to be the promised son. Now they had to live with the mess they had created. Ishmaels are real and must be cared for, even though they are not the result of faith.

You don't have to look for secret passages to follow God. His way is plain to those who will trust him. Striving to do something for him is wasted labor. He wants to do something for you that will be so obviously his own that the world will wonder at his goodness toward you.

God has made great and precious promises to his covenant people. We can rest in his trustworthiness. Jesus is the fulfillment of all God's promises to us. As we embrace his life, God performs in us everything he requires of us. When God's promises are the issue, trust and rest are the result. When principles without promises are the issue, performance and striving will always be present.

PERSECUTION VERSUS BLESSING

Third, *those who operate under the old covenant tend to persecute others, while those who live under the new covenant bring blessings to those around them.*

Someone has said that the miserable make others miserable. If so, Saul must have been a miserable man. Why wouldn't he be? He was committed to a covenant that was designed to reveal the flaws within him. He lived every day with the innate fears of natural humanity. He was painfully aware of his tendency toward lust and greed. His preoccupation with himself must have been a terrible trap.

I think I understand why Saul was so angry with these disciples of Christ who were enjoying life. They seemed so unconcerned about performing for merit. They were not self-conscious nor self-serving. They laughed a lot, even in the face of death. They were willing to die to protect fellow believers.

There was a quality about Jesus' followers that defied reason. If they were right, Saul was in a heap of trouble. They had to be stopped—and Saul was determined to stop them.

Saul of Tarsus was the epitome of the loyal legalist, bent on eradicating the heresy of Jesus from the ranks of holy Judaism. He honestly thought he was doing right by killing believers, until the revelation of Jesus on the road to Damascus. That personal encounter with a living Jesus changed him from a persecutor of believers to a preacher of the gospel. He spent the remainder of his life blessing people with the gospel of grace.

It should not surprise us when preaching the new covenant brings us persecution from those who cling to the old covenant. Typical legalists are true to Paul's description of Ishmael's treatment of Isaac and his seed: "He who was born according to the flesh persecuted him who was born according to the Spirit" (Gal 4:29).

The grace of God sounds too good to be true. It surely looks illegal to the natural mind. It is beyond any human reasoning. It can be embraced only by the human spirit as it comes by revelation. Those who are not open to revelation cannot hear it, and they take a dim view of those who can. (See 1 Corinthians 2:9-14.) But those who live under the new covenant spread its blessings wherever they go, despite the persecution of those who cling to the old.

HUMAN RESPONSIBILITY VERSUS DIVINE INITIATIVE

When you live in covenant relationship with someone, it is prudent to read the contract, especially the fine print. The Epistle to the Hebrews is a wonderful explanation of the spiritual "fine print" of the new covenant. In this letter, clear explanation is made about the purpose of the old covenant in picturing and preparing the way for the full revelation of Jesus. In chapter 8, the contrast between the two covenants is made explicit:

> Behold, days are coming, says the Lord,
> When I will effect a new covenant
> with the house of Israel and
> with the house of Judah;
> Not like the covenant which I made with their fathers...
> For they did not continue in my covenant,
> And I did not care for them, says the Lord.
> For this is the covenant...
> I will put my laws into their minds,
> And I will write them upon their hearts.
> And I will be their God,
> And they shall be my people.
> And they shall not teach everyone his fellow citizen,
> And everyone his brother, saying, 'Know the Lord,'
> For all shall know me,
> From the least to the greatest of them.
> For I will be merciful to their iniquities,
> And I will remember their sins no more. **Heb 8:8-12**

Note who does what in this new contract. And this "distribution of duties" is the fourth vital difference between the two covenants: *In the new covenant, God takes all the initiative.*

Under the old covenant, the responsibility was on human beings. They were given the standards and expected to live by them. And it was not only possible for them to fall away and utterly fail; they were assured of doing exactly that!

Under the new covenant, however, God assumes all the initiative. The old covenant implied, "If you are good enough and don't sin, you will be blessed." The new covenant says, "I will remember your sins no more." Since you can't be good enough, I will perform for you and credit it to your account.

The Book of Genesis relates an event in the life of Abraham when God makes a covenant with him (Gn 15). God tells

Abraham to prepare the animals for the ceremony. Following "standard procedure" for such a ritual, Abraham kills the animals, cuts each in two pieces, lays each half opposite the other, and waits for God to come and walk between the two halves of the slain animals with him. According to the custom of establishing a covenant, each of them would then make vows and commit to keep those vows.

But it doesn't happen that way. Abraham waits, but God doesn't come. Abraham falls asleep waiting. And then, while he's asleep, Abraham sees the presence of God walking through the slain animals for both of them. It was as if God were saying, "Abraham, you cannot keep your vows, so I will keep them for both of us. I will swear by myself that I will keep both my part and your part of the covenant."

God kept that promise through his Son, Jesus, who came to earth as both God and human, thus ultimately fulfilling his covenant vows. The pressure is not on me to fulfill any expectation, but to trust him who has taken my place.

TABLETS OF STONE VERSUS THE TABLETS OF THE HEART

A fifth contrast between the old covenant and the new is also indicated in Hebrews 8:10: "I will put my laws into their minds, and I will write them upon their hearts." In other words, *the old covenant was external, while the new covenant is internal.* The old covenant was written on tablets of stone. The new covenant is written on the inside, on the tablets of the human heart.

There is a wonderful difference between outer restrictions of law and inner constrictions of love. As we have seen, those who respond only to external laws tend to become Pharisees —rigid, judgmental, and miserable. But those who live in covenant with God not only carry the contract with them, but they are given the ability to live up to it. Inside, they know the will of God and are actually granted the desire and ability to follow it. True freedom comes as they learn to live by the desires of the God-directed inner person rather than the desires of the outer person, who was trained by the father of deception, the devil.

PERFORMANCE CONSCIOUSNESS VERSUS GOD CONSCIOUSNESS

A final important difference between the old and new covenants is *the difference between performance consciousness and God consciousness.*

Performance consciousness results from living with the old-covenant mentality. It focuses your attention on what you are producing, and it is never satisfied. The insatiable thirst of the law will drain the very life out of you. You live with the realization that it could always be done better.

God consciousness is the beautiful result of living under the new covenant of grace. God did it all. He is the initiator and the sustainer. He loves me, accepts me, forgives me, and gives me a place in his redemptive work in the world. He is the sum of all things beautiful. He possesses all the treasures of wisdom. He owns it all and is willing to share it with those who live in covenant relationship with him. Why would anyone want to be self-conscious when they can be caught up in the completeness of God himself?

IS "GRACE ONLY" AN UNBALANCED GOSPEL?

Which do you prefer—the covenant of performance, or the covenant of promise? The one that is designed to expose your nature or the one that is designed to expose God's?

To this day, people can be classified according to which of the two covenants they choose to embrace. The following chart summarizes the differences we have seen between the two covenants and those who live by them.

Old Covenant	**New Covenant**
Focus on principles	Focus on promises
Striving	Rest
Persecution	Blessing
Human beings bear responsibility	God takes initiative
Law written on tablets of stone	Law written in believer's heart
Performance consciousness	God consciousness

All of these distinctions can be summarized in a single phrase: the new covenant is the gospel of grace—absolute grace that fulfills and supersedes the law. It is the breathtaking good news: God has given us promises in place of principles, rest instead of striving, blessings instead of persecution. If we let him, God takes the initiative in our lives to change us from the inside out. We don't need to perform, only to remain open to his leading.

Does that sound too good to be true? Some people have concluded just that, and they have tried to balance the exciting good news of God's grace with the awesome warning of law. They congratulate themselves on their "balance"—but they are proclaiming a false gospel.

Grace, as expressed through Jesus, does not require any additional weight of law to bring balance. "And the Word became flesh, and dwelt among us, and we beheld his glory, glory as of the only begotten from the Father, full of grace and truth. For of His fulness we have all received, and grace upon grace" (Jn 1:14, 16).

Early in his Letter to the Galatians, Paul had pronounced a curse on anyone who would preach a gospel other than the one of grace. The legalists of his day were insisting on a mixture of the two. "Sure Jesus is necessary," they said, "but you must also keep the law." Their opinion of Jesus was, "Necessary, but not enough."

That is a cursed gospel. It is no good news at all. And it is not the gospel of the new covenant!

I was asked some years ago to be the guest speaker at a particular church that had a reputation for being rather legalistic. Strict rules about behavior and dress were enforced stringently. The pastor, however, was very open and stated that they were ready to hear about grace, for their legalism was about to strangle them.

I spoke on Sunday, and as I would make particular points about the value of grace over performance, the pastor would stand and confess, "I taught them that, Brother Hall. It is my fault; I repent and ask their forgiveness." He did that several times during my message. The people responded favorably each time, and I thought there was a wonderful relationship between pastor and congregation.

When I finished, he said, "There is so much more we need to hear about this subject. Could you come back on Thursday and speak again?" I was happy to accept.

When I arrived on Thursday, the pastor made some complimentary remarks about the previous Sunday and then said, "We have been studying about the grace of God, and we need it. But let me remind you, that is only a part of the truth. Grace must be balanced with the reality of the law and the wrath of God." All the people nodded in agreement and appreciation for a pastor who was alert enough to keep them in balance.

When I stood to speak, I simply read this verse from Galatians 4:30. "The son of the bondwoman shall not be an heir with the son of the free woman."

A stunned look came across the pastor's face. Slowly he stood and turned to the congregation.

"That's right," he said. "Grace is so fully God, it doesn't need balancing."

I wish we were all so quick to repent of our limited perceptions. I wish we all could know the fullness of living under the "unbalanced" gospel of grace.

FAITH THAT WORKS

Now, a final word on this subject of grace. Some people struggle with this point to understand the role of "works" in the life of faith. The fear of license has kept many from discovering the beauty of liberty. But such a fear reveals a deep misunderstanding of the way grace operates.

As someone long ago said, "The issue is not faith and works, but faith that works." The point is, faith comes first. We give ourselves up to God's initiative, trusting in his reconciling work. When that happens, we are granted freedom from external laws. At the same time, God writes his law on our hearts. In other words, we develop an inner motivation—based on our faith in God and our relationship with him—that inevitably shows itself in our outer lives.

When my wife tells me that we'll have dinner tonight at seven o'clock, I believe her. I trust our relationship. And I make plans to be there at seven o'clock. I arrange schedules and manage my projects according to my faith in what I've been told. But my planning and arranging does not cause dinner to be at seven; it just allows me to be there to enjoy it. In the same way, Spirit-controlled Christians will arrange and manage their lives according to their faith in what their Father has promised and thus be able to enjoy the fullness of God.

It is wasted worry, in other words, that frets over a grace that makes one lazy or licentious. Grace just doesn't work that way.

After all, was Jesus lazy? Did he misuse his freedom from the external law? I rest my case.

The new covenant is one of grace that fulfills all requirements. And that, my friends, is the gospel!

CHAPTER 13 Better than New

LITTLE KERRY BROUGHT the beautiful porcelain doll home and placed it carefully on her bedroom dresser. "I'm going to name you Katherine—after Aunt Kate," she announced.

Although Kerry had many dolls, this one immediately became her favorite—partly because of its delicate beauty, but mostly because it was a gift from her favorite aunt. Aunt Kate had carefully transported this fragile toy home from a trip around the world.

Kerry was certain that she would cherish Katherine all her life and one day have the joy of giving it to one of her own daughters. But one day, during some careless play, she accidentally bumped the dresser. The beautiful doll crashed to the floor in pieces. "Katherine," Kerry sobbed, "She's broken! She's all ruined!"

Hearing his daughter's cries, Kerry's dad came running. First he held Kerry while she wept. Then, as the sobs subsided, he said gently, "Let's see if we can fix Katherine."

After many hours of meticulous working, Dad had miraculously put the porcelain doll back together with glue. Kerry received the restored toy back with gratitude, but her comment revealed her deep disappointment. "Thanks, Daddy," she said quietly, "but it will never be the same. She used to be special. But now she's just a patched-up doll."

SHATTERED RIGHTEOUSNESS

What happens when our carefully tended lives are cracked by sin? When we make a careless or a rebellious move and all our treasured righteousness shatters? Can we be restored when we fall? Those are some of the most important questions we must pose of grace.

The standard human approach to failure seems to assume that sinners will never be anything but "patched-up" people. We look at our shortcomings with shame or embarrassment. And the standard solution is to "cover up," "make up," or "give up"—we either deny the failure ever happened, try to make up for the failure by performing good deeds, or conclude that we're second rate and can never have God's best.

But that's not the way God reacts to human failure at all! God seems neither surprised nor embarrassed by our sinfulness. In fact, he has anticipated our failings and provided for them in a wonderful way. As we look through biblical history, we find that God manifests himself through broken vessels (2 Cor 9:1-8). God has deposited his glory in "earthen vessels." He allows the vessels to be broken in order to reveal his grace to the broken vessel and to the darkness outside. He is always in the process of using what is weak for his glory.

BETTER THAN NEW

The pages of Scripture are filled with examples of human sin and failure, depicted with unflinching honesty. Eve, the first woman, is deceived. Adam chooses to disobey God. Cain murders Abel. Noah gets drunk and lies around naked. Abraham, the father of our faith, calls his wife his sister out of fear of a foreign king. Moses breaks the holy tablets in anger, strikes the rock in frustration, and is prevented from entering the promised land. Joshua neglects to get God's strategy for the city of Ai. The children of Israel refuse to believe and are left wandering in the wilderness. Saul, Israel's first king, turns out to be a maniac and ends his life in disgrace. David, the man after God's own heart, commits adultery and murder. Elijah, the great prophet of God, runs from Jezebel and hides out in the wilderness. John the Baptist, while in prison, doubts the deity of Jesus. Paul and Barnabas bicker over personnel matters. And so on and so on.

And yet look at those names again. Among them are many men and women who experienced the restoring grace of God and became heaven's heroes, expressing the glory of God on the face of the earth. All of us can thrill to the reality that God does not cull failures. He refuses to be embarrassed by human weakness, but rather uses that weakness as an opportunity to reveal his grace.

Ever since the Fall in the Garden, God has been in the ongoing process of restoring human beings to his original intent. The wonderful thing about God's restoration is that when he restores something, the restored product is better than the original! (The last Adam, for instance, is far greater than the first Adam.)

Even the Old Testament laws that governed the children of Israel were based on this wonderful truth about God's kind of restoration. When something was stolen, for instance, it had to be restored fourfold or sevenfold, depending on its category. But the climax of God's restorative efforts came in the redemptive death and resurrection of his Son. In Christ, God revealed the fullness of his restoration policy.

God never intended for fallen humans to live with continual shame because of their failure. He never intended his children to live "patched-up" lives. Instead, he made it possible for that which has been fouled or shattered to be restored to a higher state—better than new.

THE RELIGIONIST TRAP

Now this principle of brokenness and restoration is one that the religionist simply can't grasp. The legalist's goal is to follow the instructions of the Bible correctly in order to prevent sin—to get through life without ever showing any weaknesses or experiencing any failures. As a result, the religionist has no choice but to deny his or her own sin and to avoid sinners.

What happens when we fall into the trap of religionist thinking? We can't be seen with someone who has failed because some of that failure might rub off—or worse, someone might think we are failures. We begin to see weak and needy people as hindrances to the coming of the kingdom of God—nuisances that have to be tolerated rather than people to be loved. Do we scorn lost people because they act lost? Do we "tut-tut" at the down-and-out wino and flip our noses high in the air at the deceived homosexual? Do we shake our heads at the addict, and turn red with anger at fellow Christians whose mistakes hurt the church's reputation?

Isn't it strange how easy it is for us to expect sinners to act as if they aren't sinners and lost people to act as if they aren't lost—then we judge them because they don't act the way we think Christians are supposed to act? I believe one reason the church has been so ineffective in reaching the lost is that the religionists in charge refuse to meet people where they are and help them out of the mess they're in. Instead, religionists look down on sinners with disdain and disgust.

And the result? The lost remain lost. Sinners remain entrenched in their sin. And the religionists, blind to their own failings, are denied the chance for restoration as well.

GOD'S RESTORATION PROCESS: A CASE STUDY

In Jesus' dealings with a man called Simon, we see a picture of God's attitude toward success, failure, and restoration. Simon was a fisherman. One day he heard Jesus say, "Follow me," and that's what he began to do (See Matthew 4:19.) Jesus saw great potential in Simon. In fact, he began calling him by a name that described his eventual character... Peter, or "rock." (See John 1:42.)

But Peter was far from rock-like during the years when Jesus was on earth. He obviously had great leadership potential, but he struggled with glaring weaknesses as well. He was brash and overconfident yet insecure. He tended to shoot off his mouth and act without thinking.

But don't you think Jesus probably knew about Peter's weaknesses? Do you really believe Jesus was shocked when he discovered that Peter had some glaring character flaws? I think he expected incomplete people to act incomplete. Jesus called Peter knowing he had problems, but also knowing that his grace was enough to fill the gaping cracks in Peter's personality and make Peter into a vessel of honor.

All during the three-year period that Peter followed Jesus, his impetuousness got him in trouble. He tended to be aggressive, and he was usually the self-appointed spokesman for the group. Then came the night prior to Jesus' betrayal when Peter made the arrogant statement that, though all others would fail Jesus, he would not fail. (See Matthew 26:31-35; Luke 22:31-38.)

Jesus had indicated that such a time of testing was coming and that his followers would be scattered. But Peter refused to hear it. I can imagine him looking around the room, declaring his superior loyalty:

"Well, I can certainly understand your concern, Jesus, because some of these guys don't have a lot of backbone. Why, there's Judas, I've always thought he was a bit shifty-eyed. And then there's Thomas—always ready to believe the worst about a situation; he's bound to cave in. And John—I know you love him a lot, Jesus, but he sure is 'laid back' for someone involved in a great cause.... But Jesus, you don't ever have to worry about me! Yes sir, no matter what comes, when the storm is over, I'll still be on my feet!"

What an audacious display! Here's a man who's obviously not looking clearly at himself or those around him. He is blustering with self-justification and superiority, sure that he has arrived, while others are just now boarding the train. His intelligence, his personality, his ability to receive revelation, and his special experience with Jesus all have qualified him to stand head and shoulders above those around him. And he is sincere in this assessment. He really believes that when others fail he won't.

Jesus, in response to Peter's bluster, says, in essence (Lk 22:31-32): "Peter, I have some good news and some bad news for you. The bad news is, Satan has asked for permission to sift you like wheat. The good news is, he had to ask. You are not his property... you belong to me. The bad news is, I gave him permission. The good news is, I have prayed for you and all my prayers are answered. The bad news is, you're going to need those prayers. The good news is, your faith won't fail. The bad news is, everything *but* your faith will. The good news is, you're going to have a ministry when all this is over and you'll spend your life helping others."

Then comes that fateful night when Peter's "innards" are to be exposed—not for the purpose of shaming him, but so they can be cleansed by the forgiveness of the Lord and restored by his grace.

First, Jesus sets Peter up before they go to the Garden of Gethsemane.

"If you have no sword, sell your robe and buy one."

"We have two swords," somebody says.

"It is enough," Jesus says. (See Luke 22:36, 38.)

Why do you suppose Jesus asks about a sword? He has told his disciples many times before that they are not going to win this battle by fighting with the sword. So why a sword now? Could it be that Jesus wants to expose Peter's uncontrolled anger and overconfidence so it could be dealt with?

At any rate, that's what happens. When they are in the garden and the soldiers come to take Jesus away, Peter responds in true "Type A" form. He grabs the sword and tries to cut off the head of the high priest's slave, Malchus. The terrified Malchus obviously sees the sword coming and ducks, but not quite enough; the sword slices off his ear. Then Jesus picks up the bloody ear and, incredibly, reattaches it. Can you imagine how Peter must feel? His self-confident aggressiveness looks like utter foolishness in contrast to Jesus' extraordinary love. (See John 18:1-11.)

Jesus is taken off to be tried, and Peter goes to warm himself by the fire. A girl thinks she recognizes Peter's accent and accuses him of being a Galilean who followed Jesus. He denies it. She inquires a second time. Another denial. The third time he not only denies, but curses. (See Matthew 26:69-74; Luke 22:54-62.)

A little later, Peter sees Jesus being led away. Their eyes meet. And Peter's heart is smitten with grief and condemnation. This same self-confident, superior disciple has betrayed the Lord loudly and publicly—not secretly as Judas did. He has betrayed his fear and insecurity through cowardice—not in honest doubt as Thomas will do. Openly, willfully Peter has cursed and denied Jesus the Lord!

This is no minor infraction, no little indiscretion. This is big-league failure. From the human point of view, it is unmitigated disaster. From God's point of view, it is the exposure of a weakness that will prepare the way for the entrance of the grace of God! For into that giant hole in Peter's life will be poured the glory of a forgiving, restoring God who announces to a world of failures, "There's hope for you!"

Jesus appears to his disciples three times after the resurrection. There's no reason to believe Peter is not in the group at those times. But it is the third appearance of Jesus that makes the gigantic difference in Peter's life. (See John 21.)

It happens on the seashore. Jesus walks out to where the disciples are fishing. They spot the figure on the beach, and John announces that it must be the Lord. Peter, ahead of the rest, jumps in the water and splashes through the waves to Jesus.

At first we are tempted to say it's the old impetuous, self-confident Peter again. But on second glance, maybe there's more.

Can you imagine what is going on in Peter's conscience? He

has failed the Lord, and he knows it. Surely, as Peter stood in that boat, condemning voices from the inside are chiding: "Stand back. You forfeited your favored place. Stand afar off. You only deserve to be a servant, not a son."

And yet something about the risen Jesus makes Peter want to run *to* him, not *from* him. Something about Jesus makes Peter know that no one has such a claim on the risen Savior as does a failure!

If Jesus displayed any hint of legalism Peter would have wanted to take the boat further out to sea, not jump into the water in his hurry to be with Jesus. Remember, this is the third time Jesus has met with the disciples since his resurrection, and he has not even mentioned Peter's failure. How different from those who believe that perfection is the goal and sin is the focus!

The residue of performance mentality has destroyed many at the point of their failure. They have listened to those condemning voices and have stood afar off while Jesus waits on the shore with complete forgiveness and total acceptance. The grace of God teaches us that love likes to be trusted. No one honors Jesus by standing afar off, pleading unworthiness. It's bad enough to fail, but it's much worse to refuse to trust in the unconditional love of Jesus.

In the face of failure, the law-trained conscience will scream condemnation. The religionist will howl for justice and punishment. But it's the restoring grace of Jesus that bids one who has no merit to come and receive total forgiveness.

Jesus' restoration program doesn't stop with purging the conscience. It seems too much to ask that Jesus would forgive a man who had done such terrible things as denying him and cursing him. But he not only forgives Peter's failure. He also goes to the root of the problem and purifies Peter's heart.

On this occasion by the seashore, after Jesus has prepared a meal and the disciples have eaten, Jesus and Peter go for a walk, and Jesus begins gently to probe into Peter's motivations.

Now, if some religionists were watching this process of restoration, they undoubtedly would accuse Jesus of not being "tough enough" on sin. After all, this is the third time they've been together, and he hasn't even mentioned it. And now, when he could be talking seriously about failure, he is wasting his time laughing and talking and enjoying a meal.

May I encourage you not to be too hasty at accusing Jesus of not being thorough with other people in regard to their sins. Rest assured, he will finish the job. And when he is finished, not only will their foul deeds be forgiven; their impure hearts will also be purified.

Notice Jesus' conversation focuses on Peter's inner attitudes, not his act of betrayal. Jesus asks, "Peter, do you love me more than these?"

Jesus uses a word for love that is beyond Peter's ability to comprehend. Jesus actually says, "Peter, do you *agape* me more than these?" Only God can *agape*. The *agape* form of love is that unconditional, unending kind of love that comes from the heart of God. And Jesus is asking Peter whether Peter has more of that kind of love than the other disciples.

In response to such a question, Peter does the only thing he can. He responds honestly. "Yes, Lord, I love you"—but he uses a different word—*phileo*, the word for human, brotherly love.

Jesus asks again, "Do you love me the way God loves?" This time he does not add "more than these"; he asks, "Do you *agape* me at all?" Jesus wants all Peter's overconfidence exposed. He not only wants to expose Peter's notions of superiority in relation to others, he wants to know if he has any pretensions of being able to live beyond the human level.

Peter is honest again. "I love you the way a human loves."

The third time Jesus comes down to Peter's level and asks, "Do you love me the way a human loves?"

Peter's heart is exposed in stark nakedness. He cries out, "You know that I love you that way!"

Then Jesus gently responds, as he has the two previous times, "Feed my sheep."

Two things we must not miss here. First, for Jesus, the important issue in Peter's restoration was not so much the act of betrayal, but the condition of his heart. A bad heart will always produce bad behavior, and a good heart will produce good behavior. Jesus wanted Peter operating out of an honest relationship with him—not a super-inflated, deceptive relationship.

Jesus obviously has no intention of shaming Peter for the purpose of shaming him. But he does not want Peter spending the rest of his life trying to cover up, make up for, or give up on his terrible failure. So with loving, personal, probing questions, Jesus exposes Peter's heart to Peter so that the disciple can receive the forgiveness, acceptance, and restoration his Lord wants to offer.

Another thing we must not miss here is that Jesus has the audacity to take a total failure and give him the job of shepherding his precious sheep. Can you believe it? Those sheep that Jesus loved so much, those hurting human beings for whom he left heaven, came to earth, and died, he is now turning over to the care of this colossal failure. What confidence Jesus has in one who's been restored by grace!

A NEW PATH

The rest of Jesus' conversation with Peter that particular day involves the greatest personal instruction Peter has ever received.

First, Jesus explains to him what had been going on since that first day by the sea when Jesus initially said, "Follow me." He explains to Peter that all of his life he has been going where he wants to go, operating out of his own mind, ego, and desires. He had been following Jesus and doing God's work Peter's way. But from this point on, things will be different. For the rest of his life, Peter will be a follower instead of the one in charge. He won't even die the way he would choose.

Then Jesus repeats those words Peter first heard so long ago: "Peter, follow me." Peter has come full circle, having spent three years being prepared in the school of grace and truth. His weaknesses have been exposed and then covered by pure love. Now those weaknesses are being turned into strengths by the very character of God himself.

Then Jesus cautioned Peter about a temptation we all face. After Jesus has explained to Peter how his life was going to go, Peter glances up and sees John following them. And he asks that all-too-human question, "What about him?" and receives heaven's eternal reply, "That's none of your business... follow me."

When Jesus restores, he not only purges the conscience and purifies the heart, he also directs us along a new path—the path of following him. That path has no place for comparison, imitation, or competition. God gives every person a different assignment and a different set of resources to accomplish different things in this world.

GOOD NEWS FOR CRACKED POTS

God prepares his vessels through failure and restoration. When he restores, he restores fully: the conscience, the heart, the path for the future.[1] He is neither surprised nor embarrassed by our weaknesses but, because of his unsearchable fullness, he is able to take our weaknesses and make them his strengths. He pours into the gaping holes of our insufficiencies his supply, and through broken pottery he shines as the light at noonday.

We who have been restored by Jesus are not patched-up dolls. We are equipped saints, prepared not only to declare the glories of a gracious Lord, but also to demonstrate in our own lives the reality of his unfailing love. As a result, we find it difficult to look down our noses at the sinners and the failures of the world. Instead, we will view them as one of us—candidates for God's expression of grace. Something has happened in our hearts that enables us to grasp the essence of the statement, "Where sin increased, grace abounded all the more" (Rom 5:20).

1. C.H. Mackintosh, *The Mackintosh Treasury*, (Neptune, N.J.: Loizeaux Bros., 1976), 428.

CHAPTER 14 Beyond Condemnation

THE BOOK OF GENESIS contains a wonderfully refreshing statement about Abraham, the father of faith. It says that Abraham lived for one hundred seventy-five years and then died "an old man and satisfied with life" (Gn 25:8).

"Satisfied with life." What a wonderful epitaph for a person of any age! What an interesting statement to make about a man who lived as long as Abraham did and made as many obvious blunders.

If you are used to thinking about Abraham as a "Bible character" who had it all together, think again. Again and again, over the course of his lifetime, Abraham fell into cowardice, deceit, and disobedience. Twice he passed his own wife off as his sister and let her be taken by other men just to ensure his own safety. He tried to make God's promises come true in his own strength and with his own strategy. And yet he died "an old man and satisfied with life."

I wonder how Abraham found that satisfaction—how he learned to deal with regret and the condemnation of his own conscience? He obviously knew something about living above condemnation and in the confidence of his relationship with God.

Evidently few in our world have found out what Abraham's

secret is. If they had, there would be fewer frowns and more smiles. There would be fewer stress headaches and more serenity. There would be less selfishness in the world and more generosity.

In many ways, we live in a culture of condemnation—especially in our religious communities. In fact, the religionists have refined condemnation to an art form. Condemnation is used as a tool to convert people into religious behavior from heathen behavior. It is also the "weapon of choice" for shaping the consciences of the young and influencing the decisions of adults.

And the tragedy of all this is: there is no place for condemnation within Christ's church! The Bible says it plainly: "There is therefore now no condemnation for those who are in Christ Jesus" (Rom 8:1). That's an emphatic statement: "no condemnation." It just isn't there; it doesn't exist. For a person in Christ to experience condemnation, he or she would have to reach outside of Christ to get it. The liberating truth of the gospel is—no condemnation!

CONDEMNATION VERSUS CONVICTION

Is the "Yes, but..." question already surfacing in your mind? "What about conviction over sin? Doesn't God convict us when we violate our relationship with him?"

The answer, of course, is yes. Jesus promises in John 16:8-23 that the Holy Spirit will guide us into all truth and "convict the world concerning sin, and righteousness, and judgment" (Rom 16:8).

But condemnation and conviction are two different things. One leads to despair, the other to hope. One is an accusing voice, the other an encouraging voice.

Picture this in your mind: You are standing in the middle of a room. All the lights are off. The furniture is in disarray; everything is out of place. It is your responsibility to put everything in order, but every time you move, you bump into something.

That's how condemnation feels. You're in a mess, but you don't know how to fix it. You are just conscious of your failure.

Then someone turns on the light. The room is still a mess, but now you can see where you're going and how to put things right. You feel a responsibility to correct the problems in the room, but also a sense of hope and direction. That's how conviction feels.

It's a completely different set of circumstances. Conviction brings growth and is necessary to salvation, but condemnation obliterates confidence, confuses communication, paralyzes prayer, and stifles the individual. Condemnation is a tool of Satan; it is inevitably destructive. Once again, there is no place for it in the life of Christ.

LIVING WITH CONFIDENCE, NOT CONDEMNATION

The Epistle of 1 John contains a marvelously encouraging passage that helps me understand the difference between conviction and condemnation and see how I can live my life free of condemnation:

> We shall know by this that we are of the truth and shall assure our heart before him, in whatever our heart condemns us; for God is greater than our heart, and knows all things. Beloved, if our heart does not condemn us, we have confidence before God; and whatever we ask we receive from him, because we keep his commandments.... And this is his commandment, that we believe in the name of His Son Jesus Christ, and love one another.... And the one who keeps his commandments abides in him, and he in him. **1 Jn 3:19-24**

This passage makes it clear that we, as God's people, have two choices: We can live with confidence, or we can live with condemnation. God's grace has been poured out toward us, and his unconditional love has been extended to us. Now it's up to us; Do we listen to the voice of condemnation or the voice of confidence?

If you read this passage carefully, you will find that it defines confidence as the freedom to ask things of God, knowing that we will receive what we request. And this freedom is based on our relationship with God. Granted, we are told that our confidence involves keeping his commandments—but note the definition of commandments: "that we believe in the name of his Son Jesus Christ, and love one another."

We have the confidence to make requests of God because we know we are received on the basis of grace through faith—that we are his children and have the right to approach him. We have access to God through the blood of Jesus, and our standing with him is in no way dependent upon our performance or merit. There is nothing we need to do to gain acceptance into his presence. There are no unfulfilled requirements to be in right standing with him.

When we are able to enjoy God's presence on the basis of his grace, when we have the sense that we are sons and daughters, not slaves, we come often and confidently into his presence to voice our requests. We can do this because we have the assurance that we are not interrupting him or depleting his resources. We have come to understand that his greatest desire is to expend his grace toward our need. He likes nothing better than for his needy children to live in dependence on him, asking him for those things he paid much to give them. This confidence overflows into our requests.

This "asking" confidence is missing in so many of the prayers I have said and heard. Have you ever heard yourself praying something like this:

"Oh, oh God, this is... uh... Dudley Hall... and I know... uh... I really shouldn't be coming to you, but... uh... I'm in a real mess, and... uh ... I know I don't really have any right to ask anything, but... uh... I didn't know what else to do and... uh... I know that I'm selfish and... uh... probably don't know what I should be asking and... uh... with my pea-brained mind

I would never ask the right thing, so probably in your wonderful wisdom you probably won't give me what I ask for anyway, and that's probably best, so I know there's no need in asking, but I just didn't know what else to do, so... uh... good night."

Please don't think I'm making light of anyone's prayer life. I'm giving personal testimony here. But the fact is, that's not very confident praying. It's the kind of praying comes out of condemnation and doubt regarding our standing with God. Beloved children just don't talk to their father that way.

Confidence, on the other hand, flows over into our assurance that our request will be granted. When we know we are asking for the right things, we have confidence that our Father will answer appropriately. Our confidence is in his goodness, wisdom, faithfulness, and willingness to meet all our needs. We know he is not a reticent God waiting to be persuaded but a willing God who is ready to give.

THE PITFALLS OF CONSCIENCE

Confidence, we have said, is a choice. We can choose to trust our relationship with God and his promise of "no condemnation." Or we can choose to squirm in the misery of condemnation—knowing we have not done what is expected of us and feeling utterly worthless because of our failure.

Practically speaking, how do we make the choice?

First, we need to understand that condemnation usually comes through one of two channels—other people's judgments or our own conscience. (The ultimate source, of course, is the devil.) And we really can't do anything about other people's opinions, except refuse to receive them as the final word. But we can learn to live above the voice of a condemning conscience.

The conscience is that inner guide that God has placed within every human being. As we grow in the Spirit, the conscience gradually becomes conformed to the will of God. To be truly sanctified is to release one's conscience to be controlled by the Spirit of God who lives in the inner person.

But the conscience is not the same as the voice of God. Every conscience can be and has been trained by culture, tradition, and personal choice. Sadly, many people live through the dictates of their conscience rather than by the prompting of the Holy Spirit.

It's important to understand that the conscience judges by whatever standards it has been taught are right—and those standards are not infallible.

For instance, I grew up in a small town in the South where there was a "pool room"—a place where people played billiards. They also gambled, drank, and indulged in other behavior that was not healthy for a young man. My father strongly suggested that I never be caught in that wicked place, and I obeyed. Whenever I walked by the pool room, whose front window was covered with black tape, I would imagine all sorts of wickedness going on inside.

When I was seventeen, I had a date with a girl from a neighboring town. After we had been out to dinner, I asked her what she would like to do for the rest of the evening. She suggested that we go back to her home. She said she had a pool table in the garage; we could pop some popcorn and play pool.

When I heard that suggestion I felt as though I had been asked to rob a bank. "Play pool… me? Doesn't she know I'm a Christian?" Then I heard myself blurting out, "I can't do that."

As I saw the astonished look on her face, I remember thinking, "Why couldn't I do that? Are there demons in those balls? Is there something inherently wrong with the game of pool?" And yet I couldn't bring myself to take up a pool cue.

You see, I had done what many immature minds do. I associated an amoral practice with what I perceived to be an immoral place and had combined the two in my conscience. My conscience was judging on the basis of my training.

While I was doing my studies in seminary, I was called as a prospective pastor to a nearby church. The procedure for that particular church was to have me speak to the congregation, then field any questions the members might have. I was doing quite well, I thought, in answering all their philosophical and theological questions when someone in the back asked, "What's your position on 'mixed women'?"

I wanted to seem alert, responsive, and intelligent, but the fact was I had no idea what "mixed women" meant! I thought maybe the church wanted my position on racial segregation as opposed to integration. So, I began to espouse my belief that in Christ all men and women are one, that all people are created equal and should not be divided by gender, race, color, or creed.

I was stopped in the midst of my explanation. "No," the woman said, "What's your position on mixed swimmin'?"

"Oh," I thought. "That's different." But the truth is, I still didn't know what she was asking. "What is mixed swimming?" I asked myself as I tried to come up with an erudite answer. It turned out that in this particular church the question of whether the boys should swim with the girls at youth camp was a big issue. Now, I had never read in Scripture that mixed swimming particularly mattered to God. The church in which I was raised in the Southeast had not made it an issue, either. We had lived close to the coast, and boys and girls often went to the beach together without any regard as to how the church stood on mixed swimming.

So you can see, in the area of playing pool I had restrictions of my conscience. In the area of mixed swimming, I had no restrictions whatsoever, but others did. And yet, to the best of my knowledge, the Bible does not speak directly to either of those issues.

You could probably cite many other situations where the voice of conscience had little to do with the reality of God's will. The conscience is subject to faulty training. It can easily become hypersensitive or unusably dull. That's why we always get into serious trouble when we start trying to project the dictates of our conscience onto other people and force them to live according to our standards.

God doesn't want us to live under condemnation. And yet it is obvious that God wants to be actively involved in guiding our lives toward freedom and usefulness. So, how should we respond when our conscience condemns us? I would suggest two specific strategies.

1. Listen to Your Conscience. First, when your conscience speaks, pay attention. Thoughtfully consider whether your conscience is reflecting the Holy Spirit's prompting. Even if you don't think it is, don't just override the voice of conscience by violating it. That *never* works; it only produces more condemnation. If you were brought up where something was traditionally considered wrong and you tried to break free by practicing that behavior, you've probably just created guilt. Rather than producing confidence within you, it has produced confusion.

2. Appeal to a Higher Authority. The passage in 1 John gives us a wonderful revelation: when you don't like the indictment passed against you by your conscience, or when it conflicts with somebody else's conscience, your course of action is to appeal to a higher court with a greater judge. "God is greater than our hearts."

What does it mean to appeal to a higher authority? The "court" that is immediately above the conscience is the court of Scripture. If you're confused about what your heart is saying, go to the Scripture. If the Scripture speaks to that issue, then you have found the final word. If it does not, you have the privilege of appealing to an even higher court, the court of God himself. He is so interested in our walking in liberty and integrity that he will assume the responsibility of getting a verdict to us in a fashion that we can understand—whether through the wise counsel of others, the direct prompting of the Holy Spirit, or a combination of factors.

Remember Peter from the last chapter? He did a wise thing when confronted by Jesus on the seashore. Jesus kept asking,

"Peter, do you love me?" And finally, Peter answered as all of us must say when we aren't sure what our heart is telling us: "Lord, you know all things..." (Jn 21:17).

To throw oneself on the full knowledge of God is never a bad idea. To allow him to have the final verdict is always wise. You can be sure that his verdict will be higher than justice, for "mercy triumphs over justice."

Actually, however, Jesus had been giving Peter his verdict all along. Each time he asked the question, "Do you love me?" he followed Peter's response with a gentle command: "Feed my sheep." He had been trying to say to Peter during that whole experience, "I know something about you that you don't even know yourself. I wouldn't trust my sheep to someone I knew didn't love me."

Jesus was, in fact, trying to get Peter to live not by the condemnation of his conscience, but by the voice of a merciful, gracious Father.

GOD JUDGES THE INTENT

Condemnation is based on behavioral tradition—by the old elementary principle that "if I behave, I'm blessed; if I misbehave, I'm cursed." Remember, that was the essence of the old covenant that all of us were given in order to prepare us for faith. Whether consciously or unconsciously, we were all trained by these elemental principles. But that's not the way God judges! Instead, his emphasis is on *intent*.

On the six o'clock news, the TV anchorman told about an incident that had happened in a small town alongside Interstate 20 near Eastland, Texas. The highway department had dumped tons of asphalt by the roadside in preparation for some highway repair. Somehow the word had gotten out that this was surplus asphalt, and citizens would be doing the state a favor by hauling it away. So people showed up with pickup trucks, car trunks, and pasteboard boxes to relieve the state of its excess asphalt. Families received new driveways, churches got new parking lots, businesses constructed new parking areas. And then, several weeks later, the state came by and was shocked to find that all their asphalt was gone.

In interviewing the sheriff of that county about the incident, a news reporter asked, "Will there be any indictments in this case?" The old country sheriff responded, "No, there won't be any indictments. To have a crime, we would have to have criminal intent. There was no criminal intent here. People really thought the asphalt was free."

The world, the religionist, and the conscience will always be screaming for an indictment, because they are always measuring according to the technicalities of right behavior. But God always zeroes in on the intent of the heart. We too often get caught up in all the technicalities of how to do things, yet God is looking at whether or not our hearts are motivated by love and whether we are living in confident dependence on him.

There have been many times when I know I did not say the right words at the right time. There were times, as I sought to minister, when I should have been more stern, and other times when I should have been more gentle. And yet my intentions were good; in my heart, I was seeking to express love.

Because of the truth of this premise, it is not a wise idea to get into the business of judging other people. For the fact is, we can only look on the outside; only God knows the heart. Many of us would not have put up with Peter during all those years of his arrogant overconfidence, but Jesus knew that inside that brash flesh a heart was beating for truth and love.

I love the story in the Old Testament about how King David wanted to build a house for God. It was in his heart to create a dwelling place where people could come and meet God. God essentially told David that it was not the time nor was he the man to build the house—that Solomon, David's son, would build it. However, in effect, God was going to give David credit for building it, because it was in his heart to do so. In the minds of other people, David didn't get the honor of building the temple, but God gave him the credit, because God was looking at the desire of his heart.

WHEN IN DOUBT, GO LOVE SOMEBODY

The final—perhaps the most important—aspect of living above condemnation is expressing the love that has been deposited in the human spirit. John makes it clear that "if we love not only in tongue but in deed and truth, we will assure our hearts before God."

We have been taught, maybe inadvertently, that the best thing to do when our hearts condemn us is to examine ourselves, to evaluate our sincerity—basically to see if we have "done things right." But God exhorts us to reach beyond such self-evaluation.

When confusion and condemnation become your companions, seek better company! By all means, examine your motives. Weigh your conscience against a higher authority. Seriously consider whether the Spirit is convicting you of sin and urging you to repent, but refuse to get bogged down with self-evaluation and introspection. Instead, go express the love that the Holy Spirit already has deposited in you. In this expression of love, your heart will be assured before God.

One cannot receive love from God without being a repository of that love. The Holy Spirit has placed the love of God in our hearts. When confusion and condemnation become your companions, the best thing you can do is rely on that built-in supply of love and trust the Spirit to release it. When in doubt, go love somebody.

It was almost midnight when my phone rang. I heard Carol's frantic voice on the other end. Her four-year-old daughter, Melanie, was having another seizure. The doctors had not given her much hope when she had taken her to the hospital before; "Let's just hope she grows out of this," was their only encouragement. But Carol and James were horrified at the sight of their precious little girl writhing out of control, contorted by these unexplainable attacks. "Will you come and pray for Melanie?" she pleaded.

Carol couldn't have known what an awful day I had just experienced. I had been successful at absolutely nothing. I had wasted time. My plans to study and pray had been sabotaged by my own poor management. I had not communicated well with my wife and daughter. Problems at the office had depressed me. I didn't have enough recognizable faith to heal a pimple, and this dear mother is asking me to pray for a severe medical problem the doctors can't even diagnose!

"If I pray for Melanie, she'll probably die," I thought. "I need a couple of days just to get my own heart right. I'm not fit to minister to anyone. I need a weekend retreat—maybe even a full sabbatical."

"Yes, I'll be right over," I heard myself saying.

"You must be crazy," another voice seemed to say.

All the way to the Grants' house I fought those accusing thoughts. As we entered little Melanie's room, however, my thoughts began to focus on her. She was in real need, and my heart went out to her. As I joined James and Carol in laying our hands on her forehead, I knew God was interested in this situation, too. We prayed simply for quite a while. Melanie started to relax, and soon she was asleep.

"Thank you," Carol and James kept saying, "We're so sorry to have called you out so late."

"No problem, it really was my joy."

And it was! I felt great. Love had flowed through me. My mind had been distracted from me and focused on someone else. I had loved someone, and it was wonderful.

"But, what if you had not been successful? What if Melanie had not relaxed and gone quietly to sleep?" you may ask. Of course, we would have continued in our concern, but I know I wouldn't have lived under condemnation. Success is in loving, not healing. Jesus said we have fulfilled our purpose when we truly love. He is the healer, we are just the channel. This bedrock fact is the real basis for all our confidence.

CHAPTER

15 Naked in the Bushes

"THE CHIEF END OF MAN is to love God and enjoy him forever." This phrase from the Westminster Confession of Faith is a classic statement of God's creative purpose for mankind. But so few of us, it seems, have fulfilled the purpose of our creation. Too few of us know how to glorify God, and most of us are certainly not enjoying him.

What has caused us to miss the purpose of our creation so badly? Let's go back to the "Book of beginnings" to find a clue in the seminal story of humanity's creation and fall.

It is obvious that God created man for relationship with him. He didn't need any more servants; he wanted someone to love and have fellowship with. That's why he created the first man and woman as free beings—creatures who could choose their destiny. And the nature of that choice was clear from the beginning. These first humans could choose one of two trees in the Garden—the Tree of the Knowledge of Good and Evil or the Tree of Life; the tree of independence from God or the tree of relationship with God. As we have already discussed, they opted for independence.

What happened then? When Adam and Eve chose independence from God, they instantly found themselves self-conscious. They looked down and realized they were naked, and for the first time they experienced shame. Panicked, they dived into the bushes to hide.

Since that time, natural human beings have been living self-consciously. Some are conscious of how well they are doing; others are conscious of how poorly they are doing, but all are enamored of self. And just about everybody is looking for some place to hide.

All of fallen humanity has a consciousness of being incomplete and flawed. This is the result of original sin in the human race. We are imperfect in the presence of God who is absolutely perfect. So we stand vulnerable to exposure but terribly afraid.

How do we handle it? We do what Adam and Eve did; we dive behind a "bush"—scrambling for something that will cover our sense of unworthiness and shame.

God still walks through the garden of life, looking for men and women, asking the ageless question, "Where are you?" And humanity's monotonous answer—still echoing today—is, "I heard the sound of thee in the garden, and I was afraid because I was naked; so I hid myself" (Gn 3:9-10).

But can we hide from God? Of course not. How embarrassing it must have been for Adam to answer God's question while crouching in the bushes. Picture it: God asks, "Where are you?" and Adam is forced to say, "I am over here hiding behind this bush... but you are here, too, because you are everywhere and you know everything... and you really didn't have to ask that question because you knew I was here before you came looking for me...."

No, God asked "Where are you?" not for his own information, but for Adam's sake. Adam had to come out of hiding before God could begin the process of redeeming Adam's tragic choice.

We humans never emerge from behind our chosen bushes until we acknowledge we are hiding. To live in denial is to live in defeat. That's why, although God never requires performance of us, he always requires honesty. In fact, acknowledging that we have bushes we hide behind is just about all we can do. We are hopelessly and helplessly bound by fear and shame until the last Adam comes and takes the punishment for our deadly choice and makes it possible for us to receive the love of God.

But the good news is that once we admit our fear, renounce our bush, and trust his love, he removes our bush and replaces it with a vital relationship with the One who is consummate love.

WHAT'S YOUR BUSH?

We humans have spent a lot of time, energy, and money trying to disguise our bushes. We want to conceal the fact that we need a bush, but the simple fact is, we just can't face our own sense of shame without cover. We either find our own—in the form of a bush—or receive the cover God provided.

Perhaps the most popular kind of bush is that of blame. Adam and Eve found that one quickly. Adam blamed his predicament on Eve; Eve blamed it on the serpent; and, as some wag has said, "the poor serpent didn't have a leg to stand on." We've picked up on those first humans' cue and have attempted to hide our nakedness behind blame.

Blame has many faces. One of them is bitterness, which is nothing more than hiding behind other people's failures and blaming our situation on what "they didn't do right." Blame in any form has one purpose: taking the focus off me. Of course, it doesn't work; God sees through the bush of blame. Even though we have tried to shift the focus to another person or a circumstance, we are invariably left with the awful sense of inferiority and shame.

Another popular bush that men find is that of worldly success. Since human beings were created to know God and enjoy him by being a part of the family business of managing the world through love, anything less is a failure. After all, we can't go around being failures, so we find another kind of success and try to hide behind it. Maybe no one will notice what pitiful friends, spouses, parents, and Christians we are if we just accumulate enough wealth or prestige or make enough noise. So we make lots of money or become presidents of big organizations, or start a successful business or build a huge church. None of those things, in themselves, can satisfy our created purpose of knowing God, enjoying him, and showing his image to the world.

Yet another bush is intellect. If we can know enough and can communicate what we know with enough big words, maybe we can hide behind the facts.

Or perhaps we prefer the bush of verbal intimidation, which is nothing more or less than a bush used as an offensive weapon. Certainly no one would dare attack someone who is capable of mowing people down with rapid-fire, important-sounding verbiage.

What about anger? If we can keep enough fire coming through our nostrils and exude enough angry energy, perhaps we can prevent people from seeing how really insecure and weak we are.

Then there's the bush of busyness. Oh, how convenient this bush has been—a savior for many a self-conscious soul. If we stay busy answering phones, writing letters, holding meetings, serving on boards, going places, and doing things, surely people will think we are important. Maybe no one will see how badly we have failed in knowing God and enjoying him, displaying his image, and ruling the world through love.

The biggest bush in the garden—the one that hides more people than any other—is the bush of religion. It's a respected bush, covered with all the outward symbols that speak of purity, holiness, and divinity. But if all our religion does is hide our nakedness and shame, it is nothing more than a bush, and it certainly does not impress God.

To those who have used this particular hiding place, doctrine is a favorite part of the religion bush. Think of all the defensiveness and downright aggression over "doctrine" in the church. For centuries, particular doctrinal emphases have been bushes that were used to protect human self-consciousness; many private and public wars have been fought over nonessential doctrine.

Of course, there are doctrines central to Christian faith that cannot be compromised—such as one God expressed in three persons, salvation in Jesus alone, the divine inspiration of the Bible. But as we have seen, these central doctrines are seldom the ones singled out to defend. Usually, a doctrinal war is fought over some emphasis that is not that essential.

Maybe this can help us understand better why people have been willing to kill or be killed for the sake of doctrinal preference. For these people, doctrine is not just a truth to live by, but a bush that guards their shame and protects their nakedness. Doctrines that bring life-giving energy to the believer do not have to be defended. In fact, if a doctrine must be defended with violence and controversy, in all probability it is just a bush.

TEARING AWAY THE BUSHES

We can't really hide behind bushes, of course; in the long run, they just don't work at hiding our nakedness and shame. Hiding behind bushes inevitably cramps our style. Who can live in freedom when our muscles are cramped by crouching?

But let me ask you: If you were naked in a public place and the only cover you could find was a bush, how would you respond to someone who tried to take that bush away? How would you react to someone who assured you that the bush just didn't do the job and then proceeded to pull you out from behind it and into public view?

You know what you would do. You would fight!

It's amazing how attached we become to our bushes. If anyone tries to tear them down, we come unglued. According to our perverted perceptions, we can't live without our bushes.

I was raised in the rural South. Many churches in the area where I grew up had baptismal pools concealed under the pulpit platform. When it was time for baptism, they simply moved the pulpit, opened up the floor, and poured in the water. Often they would hang curtains on each side of the front so the men and women could change clothes separately.

One Sunday night, in one of these churches, a woman was being baptized. As she was lowered into the water, she slipped. She reached behind her to grab onto something solid. But what she grabbed, unfortunately, was the curtain surrounding the men's dressing room. The curtain fell. And there, in all his nakedness, stood the next baptismal candidate. Panicked, he clutched for something to hold in front of him. The nearest thing he could find was a straight-backed chair. So there he crouched, holding the chair in front of him, with this awful look of horror on his face.

One of the deacons of the church, seeking to help the situation, ran to the back of the building and switched off the light. The nervous, rumbling giggle of the congregation went on as five interminable minutes passed. Finally, believing that the poor man had been given enough time to get dressed, the deacon switched on the light. And there, paralyzed by his fear, was the man—still crouched behind the chair. I suppose he just wasn't sure when the light would be turned back on!

Now, let me ask you, what would have happened if you had gone up and tried to take the chair away from that man? You know exactly what would have happened; he would have fought with all his energy. That's the way we humans will fight to keep our bushes.

People will never be coerced into coming out from behind their bushes. This is something the church must learn if it is ever going to be effective in sharing the gospel with a self-conscious and terrified humanity. Every human in the world has found something that, to some degree, covers his or her nakedness, and that person is not going to give up that covering; the shame would be too unbearable. When the immature church tries to tear down the bushes that give men their security, no matter how inadequate those bushes may be, the church will fail.

There is a solution to the problem of hiding behind bushes. All the "fire and brimstone" preaching in the world can't do what love will do.

When Adam and Eve sinned and their nakedness was exposed, innocent blood had to be shed to take care of the problem. God took the life of an innocent animal and covered their nakedness with the skin.

That solved the external problem, but of course it didn't resolve the inner reality of shame and rebellion. In fact, if you keep reading Genesis 3, you will discover that, because of their sin, Adam and Eve had to leave the garden.

But the problem was straightened out eventually. Several thousand years later there was another Adam who chose not the Tree of the Knowledge of Good and Evil, but the Tree of Life. He lived approximately thirty-three years on earth in a vital, dependent relationship with the Father. He enjoyed God and expressed perfect love on the earth. Then, when the time came, he assumed the guilt of the first Adam and all of his descendants.

The second Adam, too, was made to leave the garden, even though he himself had no guilt. In doing so, he paid the price of separation and isolation and fear. He made it possible for all of Adam's descendants to come into a relationship of life with God. He was demonstrating the only eternal agent of change in the world... love!

The apostle John later penned these words, "perfect love casts out fear" (1 Jn 4:18). Human beings will never come out from behind their bushes by coercion. Only love will bring them out.

God has no part in snatching down men's bushes in order to shame them. But he has done a complete work in making it possible for human beings to walk out from behind our bushes, in all our nakedness, and be eternally covered by unconditional, unending love.

INEXPLICABLE LOVE

"Perfect love casts out fear," but perfect love is difficult to comprehend.

For one thing, perfect love—God's love—has no exceptions. "For God so loved the world," wrote John, "that he gave his only begotten Son." The world—that's everyone. If you live in the world, perfect love is offered to you. It is not offered only to the good. It is not offered on the basis of merit or pity. Only the needy get special consideration, and every one of us is needy.

In addition, perfect love has no basis except the nature of the lover. There is absolutely nothing inherent in humankind that should make God love us. For instance, God did not look into the future and see that you were going to do good, then decide that he would love you. He loved you because he is full of love. Loving is his nature; he is only acting consistent with himself. If that doesn't make sense to the rational minds of Adam's descendants, it is because such love is a divine thought and must be received by faith.

Another reason perfect love is difficult to comprehend is that it has no end. Since there is no human basis for its beginning, there is nothing we can do to end it. God's perfect love is eternal love. It can't be earned by what you do nor forfeited by what you don't do. You can choose to receive it, or you can choose to ignore it, but you can't end it. God will not force you to enjoy his love, but you can't stop him from offering it.

Here is a promise to you: Every time you choose to embrace love, another bush will fall away, another encumbrance will be annihilated, so you can walk in a new measure of freedom.

When we finally get tired of crouching behind our bushes, defending them, and trying to peer through the leaves, we can come out from hiding. Just as Adam and Eve were clothed in the skin of a slain animal, Adam's descendants can come from behind their bushes, clothed in the righteousness of the slain Lamb, Jesus.

I am constantly amazed at how simple and direct God is in dealing with his people. Think of this simple statement: "You shall know the truth, and the truth shall make you free" (Jn 8:32). That means that if there is any bondage in our lives, somewhere, consciously or unconsciously, we have internalized an inaccurate definition of reality. We have taken a lie as truth, and that lie brought darkness and bondage into our lives. The only cure for this dark condition is to hear the truth. And here is the truth: "Perfect love casts out fear."

If, in fact, I am correct in my evaluation that humanity's key problem since the fall has been fear and self-consciousness—then the only solution is to receive perfect love. When we do that, we enter into a relationship with Jesus, who is the fullness of truth. In this relationship we have marvelous fellowship as he redefines reality for us and speaks his life into us. And in the process, the problems that have hounded man throughout history are taken care of. The truth has set us free and love has cast out fear.

No wonder the apostle Paul exhorts believers to speak "the truth in love" (Eph 4:15) in our relationships with each other. In so doing, we help liberate each other from the bushes. Unhindered by the bushes, we are free to step out into the garden, to know God and enjoy him forever, and to rule this created earth through love!

CHAPTER 16 Married and Miserable

THIS CHAPTER IS NOT ABOUT your sister and brother-in-law whose marriage is a ten-year-old fight. It is about those who have been married to the law—and that's all of us.

We didn't really have any choice about this union. As God's creations, born into his world, we were betrothed to the law before we were able to give our own consent. The law is engraved in our nature. It is amplified by every institution of society. Our parents rewarded us for good behavior and punished us for bad. We received good grades in school when we performed well and low grades when we performed poorly. We receive higher wages in the marketplace when our performance merits it. If we are faithful in the activities of the church, we are given positions of importance. We even have a high self-esteem when we do well and fccl inadequate when we perform under par.

All that is part of being under the law. Like marriage, it's a "till death do us part" commitment. That's what the apostle Paul tells us in Romans 7; he uses the marriage relationship to illustrate and explain the union of humankind and the law. Let's follow Paul's lead and use a little allegory to understand this dynamic.

MARRIED TO THE LAW

Let's say that Susan Peoples is married to Jason Law. At first Susan is really excited about the challenge of being married to Jason and spending her life pleasing him. She loves him. She respects him. She really does want to make him happy, and she is smugly certain that she can.

It's not long, however, before married bliss turns into self-conscious strife and misery. The problem is, Jason just can't be satisfied. He believes it is his job to point out every flaw in Susan's character. He questions her every move and examines her every motive.

Susan works hard to improve. After all, she knows that she isn't perfect and that marriage requires adjustment, but Jason is relentless. He never mentions her improvement, only her failures.

When Susan married Mr. Law, she really thought she could make the union work. She wasn't aware that Jason's very nature required him to reflect the wickedness and weakness of her character back to her.

What a happy thought! Imagine being married to someone whose very existence is predicated on pointing out your failures. But this is exactly the purpose of the law. It defines sin for us and shows us ourselves with brutal honesty. More specifically, it defines the boundaries of "right" so we will know when we trespass.

Have I told you about my ability as a tennis player? Well, I'm one of the greatest. I can hit all types of shots—service, forehand, backhand, top spin, slice, everything. In fact, only one thing limits my game. When they draw those boundary lines on the court and put up that net, my ability is quickly redefined. I am great only when there is no "out of bounds." Those rules make the game more fun, but they really do reveal the limits to my expertise as a tennis player.

Paul said, "I would not have come to know sin except through the law" (Rom 7:7). God did not want us to live forever as deceived, sinful, lost people, so he gave us the law to reveal our need of something beyond ourselves.

The law really is good. It allows us to view life's externals the way God does. That is why Susan's marriage to Jason Law looks so promising in the beginning. However, Susan's feelings begin to change as she recognizes the fact that, although Jason's standards are absolutely just, she is simply incapable of meeting them. No wonder her excitement turns to misery and despair!

It's not long before Susan begins to experience other feelings as well. Not only does she feel deeply inadequate; she grows angry and rebellious. She finds herself doing things deliberately to irritate Jason. To her dismay, Jason just reflects back to her these ignoble attitudes.

For that's another thing law does. Not only does it draw the lines to define the boundaries; it also incites the rebellious heart to go beyond those lines.

Have you ever been on a diet? Well, I have. I remember one in particular which clearly spelled out the proper food choices. I was reading over my possible menus for the day and, honestly, they weren't too appetizing. So I flipped the page to the section entitled "Foods to Avoid." One of those items was asparagus with cheese.

Now, as far as I can remember, I have never had a craving for asparagus with cheese. Ice cream with chocolate sauce, maybe —never asparagus with cheese. But once apprised of this prohibition, I suddenly developed a powerful yen for cheese-covered vegetables. All day I yearned for some beautiful asparagus topped with golden cheddar. The trees reminded me of the asparagus; each cloud in the sky spoke loudly of the creamy cheese. The boundary line was not only marking off the court; it was calling me to jump over. The thing I knew I should not have became the thing I desired most.

As the father of two children, I have had a lot of experience attempting to remain sane at birthday parties for five-year-olds. I have learned to amuse myself—ideally, without diminishing the kids' enjoyment—by suggesting new games. One of these is grossly named "The Spit Game." Here is how it works: First, I gather the kids together and welcome them to the party, saying, "Kids, you're so welcome here. Thank you for accepting our invitation to celebrate David's fifth birthday. I want you to have a good time, so here are some suggestions. There is a big yard to play in, and it is full of great toys. You can climb the trees. You can jump on the trampoline. You can romp with the dogs... we really do want you to have fun. In a little while, we will have some cake and ice cream. David will open his presents, and there will be party favors for everyone. But there's just one thing. Do you see that flower bed right over there? No one is to spit in the flower bed. You understand that, don't you? Absolutely no one is to spit in that flower bed. Now go and have a good time."

You already know what will happen. Little kids who have never spat before develop a desperate need to spit. Saliva begins to flow at an unprecedented rate. Those little kids are going to drown if they can't spit. And sure enough, one of them will finally succumb to the overwhelming temptation. The flower bed will get watered.

What is this phenomenon? It is the law at work, inciting rebellion even as it reveals the human heart. Most people think sin is only a violation of a stated law of God. They never know how enticing sin is until they try living up to the law. Then they learn the hard truth that *sin is a heart condition.* Part of the law's purpose is to expose that truth—"that sin might become utterly sinful" is the way Paul puts it (Rom 7:13).

THE ONLY WAY OUT

Well, what is Susan going to do? She is married to Mr. Law and he continually exposes her sin—inside and out. She's married and miserable. What are her options?

Can she divorce him? That won't work. You see, Jason Law

is adamant that Susan is bound to him until death.

Some people do try to "divorce the law" by simply choosing to live apart from it. They just pretend there isn't a law, and try to live in freedom. Eventually they all testify that denial won't erase the union with Mr. Law.

Death! That's the answer. What if the law dies? Will that work? Wouldn't Susan be free if Jason Law died?

Two problems there. First, Jason is righteous and good and does not need to die, but more to the point, he is eternal and *can't* die (Rom 7:12).

Susan is caught in a sticky predicament. She is miserably married to Jason Law, who is determined to expose everything about her that is sinful. The only way out of the marriage is death, and he can't die. What is she going to do now?

Well, she could die. Some solution! A lot of good that will do her.

But here's one more possibility—one that moves the whole story beyond the simple marriage scenario and to the realm of the eternal. What if someone came and took Susan's place in her marriage to Jason Law? What if that person fulfilled his every demand so that, in the mirror of Mr. Law's eyes, there was nothing sinful to reflect? What if that person died and paid the penalty required of those who break the holy law, then was raised from the grave to a new life?

Finally, what if that person said to Susan, "You can be free of your marriage to Jason Law on one condition—that you will accept my death as yours, my burial as yours, and my resurrection as yours, and be totally united with me in covenant marriage. That is the only way out. You can't just get out of your marriage to Mr. Law and be single and independent. Only by death and remarriage can you be free."

Some have defined grace in terms of the law's dying. They've tried to make Jesus' death on the cross the crucifixion of the law. Then they thought they were free to live any way they wanted without any restrictions or penalties. But surprise! It just doesn't work that way. Jesus made it very clear that he had no intention of abolishing the law. (See Matthew 5:17.)

Others have sought to explain grace in terms of Jesus' coming to Susan and helping her live up to the demands of Mr. Law. But that doesn't work, either. As long as she stays married to the law, even with Jesus' help, she will continue in her miserable self-consciousness.

So Susan dies with Jesus, is resurrected, and is united with him in covenant love. She is dead to the law. She no longer has to cringe at the reflection of her flaws, because she is gazing only at Jesus. Because she is his, she sees that his perfection is hers, too. As long as she looks only at her new husband, she will be conscious only of him and will reflect the glory of his face. "But we all, with unveiled face beholding as in a mirror the glory of the Lord, are being transformed into the same image from glory to glory, just as from the Lord, the Spirit" (2 Cor 3:18).

LEARNING THE LANGUAGE OF LOVE

Now Susan faces a struggle in her new life. After all, she was married to Jason Law for a long time, and he trained her well in the ways of being a loyal wife. Her definition of commitment came from him. Her perception of her duty as a marriage partner was instilled by him. She still thinks "law thoughts."

When Susan communicated with Jason, the topic was always what needed to be done and what she had done wrong. So she finds it strange to listen to her new husband, who talks in terms of love and intimacy. She keeps trying to bustle around, fulfilling her wifely duties, while he is trying to tell her of the wonders he has prepared for her. It takes awhile for her ears to become attuned to the voice of grace and love.

It is natural for us who have been married to the law to expect God to speak to us only in commands. Sometimes we miss out on intimate fellowship because we just can't hear his statements of love. We may even believe that "God doesn't speak to me." If he is speaking the language of love and you are tuned in to hear only the language of law, he might as well be speaking Hebrew.

Some people, in fact, have actually studied Hebrew for the specific purpose of hearing God better, only to discover they had more information, not more revelation. Studying Bible languages is a wonderful discipline and will aid anyone in Bible study, but by itself, it will not open your ears to the voice of God when he speaks in love's language.

Have you ever noticed how many commands are given in the first eleven chapters of Paul's letter to the Romans? Not many! I realized that recently as I taught Romans to some young disciples who were accustomed to "doing something" for God. As the class progressed, they became very frustrated at discovering that for several chapters there was nothing for them to do. In fact, there are no imperative verbs (commands) in the first five chapters.

Only in Romans 6:11 do we find a command: "Consider yourselves to be dead to sin, but alive to God in Christ Jesus." And that command calls for an act of faith, not of feet. It certainly doesn't require a lot of physical energy. (Of course, it is no accident that this command comes first in this great treatise. If "dying to sin" is not accomplished first, all the subsequent commands will be carried out in the flesh and will be nothing more than religious activity.)

There are a few more imperatives in Romans 6 concerning how we are to "consider ourselves," but no more in chapters 7, 8, 9, or 10. Finally, a couple of commands crop up in chapter 11; they relate to pride in the elective grace of God. But that's it—in eleven whole chapters, fewer than five commandments.

Now think about this relative lack of commands in a major biblical message. Do you get the impression that your new husband wants you to know something about your relationship before you try to fulfill his commands? That's exactly what's happening! Jesus wants to retrain you in the language of love before you go out to expand the family business.

Oh, there are plenty of imperatives in chapters 12 through 16. There is much for you to do, and Jesus is interested in your doing it the best way possible. He has wisdom about every aspect of life and he will share that wisdom with his lover if given a chance.

There is interesting news for anyone who fears that the emphasis being put on intimacy will result in less productivity. Just the opposite is true; children will be born of this marriage. Those who marry Jesus after dying to the law will "bear fruit for God" (Rom 7:4).

Fruitfulness is not to be our first concern. In fact, "fruit consciousness" is a part of the legalistic mentality. Jesus never said that our job was to bear fruit; he said that our responsibility is to abide in him. (See John 15:4.) But if we do abide in him, fruit will be a natural by-product.

Jesus' analogy of the vine and the branches suggests that the vine, Jesus, is the one who actually produces the fruit. The branches—that's us—will bear the fruit. We need not strain at the production. Just stay put... attached to the vine. An honest look at history will reveal that those who have made an impact for good on our society have not been the ego-motivated people of performance, but the love-motivated people of faith.

HOLY ADULTERY!

This is a terrible thought, but what if—after all she and Jesus have been through together—Susan begins to think about Jason again. Maybe she reads the books he wrote or begins to fantasize about their life together. Her loyalties begin to shift back to Mr. Law. How would you label Susan's actions? I would call it adultery! In her heart, Susan is being unfaithful to her new husband.

This happens to many who have entered by faith into this

new realm of living. They break faith with the One who has saved them and revert to living under the law. Their experience is one of "falling from grace." But they haven't fallen into hell. They have fallen into law, and they are as miserable as Susan was before her death and resurrection.

These "holy adulterers" (who really are far from holy) have tasted the liberty of an intimate love life, but for some reason they have retreated to a former concept of pleasing God. As a result, they are experiencing all the fruit of the legalistic mentality: feelings of inadequacy and condemnation, fear of failure, people consciousness, judgmentalism, and joylessness.

If they remain in this state long, they will begin to doubt if they were ever really converted. They will be easy targets for the Enemy's fiery darts of accusation. Or they may be manipulated by religious leaders who will take advantage of their vulnerable state. They can quickly become another scalp on the belt of one who is caught in the religious "numbers game."

Consider this scenario. John is a relatively new Christian who is zealous to be righteous. Somehow he becomes focused on the law again. He experiences the debilitating results of law living and begins to doubt his salvation. Then someone suggests that he probably didn't "do it right." Maybe he didn't pray the right prayer. Or maybe he wasn't sincere enough. Or maybe he didn't do enough to keep his faith vibrant.

"Why not do it right this time?" some well-meaning friend recommends. So John tries to be born again... again. But this time his focus is on technically "doing it right." And nothing happens, because you can't be born through what you do.

Poor John! He is so confused. He has forgotten who he is married to. No wonder he feels defeated!

Or what about Jane? She has heard that the Christian life is not easy, but she resolves to put as much into it as she can. After all, she learned to ride a bicycle by working at it. Why can't the Christian life be approached the same way?

Jane's Christian experience is reduced to a series of formulas, steps, and "keys to success." She doesn't have much patience for those who won't work at their faith. In her mind, there are principles to live by; anyone can live the Christian life "right" if he or she tries hard enough, so "get going" is her motto.

Of course, Jane is not doing too well in some areas of her private life, but she can't admit that to anyone. She must keep propagating her gospel. There is a world to win, and no time to squabble about some inconsistencies she can't fix. She continues to give out her tracts. But nobody seems to read them—they've read her eyes instead. Jane is successful by the law's standards, but she evidences no joy in her life. There is none of that unexplainable aura that is around people passionately in love.

Jane tries to lose herself in service, but she dreads those silent times when she is alone with her thoughts. She wouldn't think of missing a church service, but in times of stark honesty she admits they're not much fun. She studies her Bible regularly and takes copious notes, but she doesn't hear her "lover's" voice anymore.

Jane, too, has fallen from grace into law. She has committed adultery against a husband who loved her enough to die for her.

Adultery is a serious sin. Even the perverted world looks upon marital infidelity as a big problem. How much more serious when the sin is against Jesus himself? No wonder the Enemy would like to keep us distracted with sins against the law—the "thou shalt nots"—when the sin that is wrecking our lives is that of spiritual adultery.

Have you noticed that you can tell if someone is focused on the law or on the Lord by listening to that person's definition of sin? The law defines sin in terms of violated *rules*, but grace defines sin primarily in terms of violated *relationships*.

For instance, the major sin of God's covenant people is that of unbelief. That is not too hard to figure out, since God's primary requirement is faith. In fact, I would dare say that no violation of the law is ever committed until unbelief is exhibited.

And what is unbelief but a rupture in a person's relationship with God?

Picture a man standing with his right hand extended toward heaven, receiving from his Father everything he needs for life and godliness. As long as his hand is open, God fills it with everything he needs to satisfy every legitimate desire.

Now imagine that something causes that man to close his hand. What happens? The supply from heaven stops... but the desires continue. The man has legitimate desires that are crying out for fulfillment.

Enters the Tempter. He is on the other side, offering satisfaction through illegitimate means. He paints beautiful pictures of how wonderful things can be if his way is chosen. Pressed by his need, the man reaches out his left hand to partake of the offerings of sin.

But take careful note: The man refused the grace before he yielded to the temptation. All other sins are preceded by spiritual adultery—the sin of broken faith with the One who put his life on the line for us.

Well, what can be done about this horrible sin of adultery and unbelief? Repentance! Coming clean. And it is better than you can imagine.

Repentance is the process of exposing darkness to light, lies to truth. Honesty before God brings us his undivided attention—and his forgiving love. We can't climb our way out of the pit. But when we admit we are in the pit and call for help, the God of grace and truth will deliver us from its deception and destruction.

Scripture reminds us: No temptation has overtaken you but such as is common to man; and God is faithful, who will not allow you to be tempted beyond what you are able, but with the temptation will provide the way of escape also, that you may be able to endure it (1 Cor 10:13).

And because of that promise, we can pray with confidence:

"I have sinned against you, my Lord, by going back to a former relationship and focusing my attention there. I was wrong. Thank you for showing me my deception and forgiving me of my sin. I have fallen from grace and into the law. I have been preoccupied with myself and not with you. Please restore our relationship. I fully receive you as my only love."

Try it! It works.

CHAPTER

17 Ministry without Manipulation

I WAS REALLY FEELING GOOD that day as I drove past the car dealership—that is, until I decided to drop in. Let me tell you how it happened.

A few days before, I had finally decided to purchase a car for my wife to drive. I had weighed all the obvious options and spent time in prayer. I felt confident God had given the go-ahead—it was time to get the car.

Now, over the years I had been through this process a time or two, and I knew the car sales game. In an effort to avoid the gamesmanship, I had called a friend who owned a dealership and asked if I might work directly with the manager. My friend had referred me to Curtis, the manager, who carefully listened to my description of the specific kind of car we had decided to buy. Curtis had told me he did not have that particular car on the lot, but would keep on the alert. He had promised to call me as soon as the right car became available.

But that day, on my way home from the office, I realized I had about thirty minutes before my next appointment, so I decided to drive by the lot just to see if my special car had come in. As I drove onto the lot, I was met at my car by an eager salesman. He was doing all the things that good salesmen do, and I was trying to be polite.

"Good afternoon, my name is Dave. May I help you?"

"Not really. I've come to see Curtis. He and I have already talked, and he knows exactly what I'm looking for."

"Well, Curtis is not in right now," said Dave, "but I'll be happy to show you anything we have, and I'm sure I can make you happy. Exactly what kind of car were you looking for?"

I explained to him exactly the kind of car I had discussed with Curtis—and again asserted that I would prefer to wait until Curtis was available.

"Please don't leave," said Dave. "This is my first day on the job, and if you leave before I get your name and address I'll be in serious trouble. You wouldn't want me to get into trouble, would you?"

I was fairly sure this was not his first day on the job, but being the kind person that I am, I agreed to give him my name and address.

Dave beamed. "Why don't we just step into my office," he coaxed. "It's much cooler in there. I'll just get all this information, and then I will turn it over to Curtis when he returns."

"I have an appointment in twenty minutes," I told Dave. "I really don't have time to go into your office. Just let me give you my name and address, and you can tell Curtis I dropped by."

"Please, I promise to let you out in time to make your appointment. But I must do this properly or I will get into trouble," pleaded the salesman.

While sitting in his office filling out his form, Dave's supervisor came in.

"Mr. Hall, exactly what kind of car were you looking for?"

"I've already explained that to Dave," I said, but I courteously went over the description again.

"We don't have one exactly like that," he said, "but we have one that comes very close. It's out back. Would you come out and look at it with me?"

"I really don't have time," I said. "I have an appointment in ten minutes, and I just came by to speak to Curtis."

"Please," he said, "it will only take a moment. Let me just

show you what we have, and then you can be on your way."

Uncomfortable now that my plans had been derailed, I hurriedly looked at the car and made the mistake of admitting it was nice.

"Good, then you could be satisfied with this car," said the manager, with Dave looking over his left shoulder.

"I suppose I could," I said, "but I really don't have time to make a deal today. I have an appointment in five minutes."

"We have this car on a special consignment from another dealership, and I think I could give you a really good price on it if we can make a deal today. Would you please just sit down in my comfortable office while I make a quick call to the other dealership?"

While waiting impatiently in his office, I realized I was going to miss my appointment, so I called my wife and asked her if she would cover for me. A minute later, into the office walked Dave, his supervisor, and the representative from the other dealership.

"You came in at just the right time, Mr. Hall," said Dave's supervisor. "I believe we can make a deal today that would be very pleasing to you. Would you please just take a ride with Dave and see what you think about the car?"

Since I had already missed my appointment, I decided I might as well make the best of this botched plan and find out as much information as I could, so I took the ride. I arrived back at the office and was met by the group of salesmen, all wanting to know what I thought.

"It's a nice car," I said, "but I really don't want to buy today. I really just came by to see Curtis...."

"What would it take to put you in that car today, Mr. Hall?" asked Dave's supervisor.

"I don't *want* to be in that car today," I said. "I don't have the time to be making this kind of decision. I do appreciate your showing it to me, but I'll have to get back with you."

"Don't leave, Mr. Hall," said Dave. "I'm sure we can work out something today that would please you. How much would you be willing to give for this car?"

I had previously done some homework on this model, and I had a good idea what the market value was. So, I chose a figure several hundreds of dollars less than what I thought their bottom price would be.

"Oh, Mr. Hall, please," he said. "You know we can't do that."

"Very well," I said. "That's my offer, and now I must go."

"Please be fair," said one of the trio. "You must understand that we have to stay in business."

"I do understand," I said, "and I do want you to stay in business. But that's my offer. If it's not satisfactory, then I really must go."

I walked out of the office and headed for my own car. Just as I was unlocking the car door, I suddenly heard these words.

"Congratulations, Mr. Hall, you just bought yourself a car!"

I haggled for another hour and a half over such internal features as the radio and the tape deck. Then I headed for home—two and a half hours later than I had planned—with my purchase. I drove the new car into the garage, walked straight into the house, and sank down into a chair, limp and lifeless. My eyes were glazed over and I felt totally empty.

Now, normally when I buy something, I'm really excited, and can't wait to play with my new "toy." When I buy a new fishing lure, I fill the bathtub with water and run my lure back and forth with my hands, just to see how it works. If I buy a new shirt, I tear open the package and wear it around the house. And yet, on this day, after I had just made a major purchase, I had no enthusiasm. What was wrong with me?

As I slumped there in the chair, I thought of one of my recent speaking engagements—one that just hadn't gone well. I had given that church all that I had in terms of concentration, energy, and love. I had done the very best speaking I knew how to do, trusting the anointing of the Holy Spirit to minister life. Yet the people had sat there, night after night, with a glaze over their eyes. They were very courteous, and they would come by after each session and compliment me on my communications skills—but I could tell that nothing was getting through. "What's wrong with these people?" I had prayed, but at the time I had received no answer.

Now as I sat in my own house, my own eyes glazed over and my own body limp from lack of energy, I understood what was wrong with those people, as well as myself. They had been "numbed" by years of manipulative ministry. I had been "had" by the world's salesmanship. But we both had the same symptoms. In a sense, we had been bewitched.

BEWITCHED AND BEWILDERED

Bewitched. Paul uses that term to describe what had happened to the Galatians (Gal 3:1). Illegitimately controlled, manipulated, forced to act contrary to the normal procedure, intimidated, victimized—all of these, and more, describe the experience of being bewitched.

The Bible says that rebellion is as the sin of witchcraft (1 Sam 15:23, ASV). Rebellion, in its essence, is choosing an order other than God's order. It is not, as some have supposed, the refusal of any order—that would be anarchy. Rebellion submits to an order, but it's an order other than God's choice. Any time a person is enticed to act outside of the order designed for him by God, he is being bewitched.

The people in Galatia were being coerced to act in a way contrary to the covenant they had made with God. They had entered into a covenant of grace with God through Jesus Christ, a covenant which stated that their sins were forgiven, that the law of God had been placed in their hearts and minds, that God had totally identified with them as his people and had given them knowledge by revelation. But now they were being encouraged by some legalists to operate under another covenant altogether. They were being told that unless they operated according to the old covenant with its focus on external behavior, they were not truly people of God.

It is obvious that the Christians in Galatia understood the reality of Christ's crucifixion and resurrection. They knew what was purchased for them on the cross and what they had won through Christ—victorious life. They had already received the gift of the Holy Spirit, probably accompanied by signs. They had already had the opportunity to suffer for their faith, and they had experienced miracles from God.

In other words, the Galatians were genuine New Testament Christians—and yet they were vulnerable to being bewitched. They were being forced back into an Old Testament, external-covenant mentality, manipulated by a group of legalists into choosing an order contrary to God's way of doing things.

The apostle Paul was not very kind to these manipulators. In fact, he wrote that anyone who preaches a gospel contrary to the gospel of grace is operating under a curse!

But despite Paul's renunciation, legalistic manipulation has worked its way into today's Christian ministry, reproducing itself under the respected reputation of religion. Old Testament externalism has been imposed on New Testament believers. People are persuaded to keep the law through the threat of punishment and the offer of blessings. Fear, guilt, greed, ambition are invoked as motivations to accomplish spiritual goals. Many people—even regular churchgoers like the ones to whom I spoke—have been manipulated to such a degree that they can't even hear the good news of the gospel of grace.

THE TRAP OF MANIPULATION

For centuries, misguided Christian ministers have used the methods of the world to motivate believers to behave in a particular way. Any appeal to mere human virtues such as sympathy, kindness, or generosity discounts the fact that a new-covenant Christian must operate out of his spirit. This is not to say that human virtues are bad, but that they are beside the point when it comes to spiritual motivation. The whole purpose of the new covenant is to build up the inner person so that the believer operates first of all out of the spirit, in obedience to God's promptings. But manipulative, bewitching ministry ignores that bedrock truth and appeals instead to our untrustworthy human emotions.

In case you're beginning to think, "Well, this chapter doesn't pertain to me; it's just for those in the professional ministry, think again. Remember, *all* of us are called to be ministers. All of us are called to witness to others, to make disciples, to build up our fellow Christians, to participate in the work of the church. And all of us—whether we are professional preachers, office staff, committee members, teachers, or clean-up crew—can fall into the trap of using manipulation to further our ministry goals. Whenever we take seriously the task of promoting the gospel, we become vulnerable to promoting it the wrong way.

What are some of the standard tactics of manipulative ministry? Some ministers have sought to further the goal of proper religious behavior by setting someone up to be embarrassed if he or she does not comply. For instance, have you ever been manipulated into giving money only because you do not want to be embarrassed by not giving?

I can remember an occasion when a particular church I attended was raising money for a building project. My wife and I, along with a number of other couples, were invited to a very nice banquet sponsored by a fund-raising organization.

At the banquet, I noticed that all the couples were essentially in the same age group and socioeconomic stratum. We all had about the same number of kids, of the same age, and we all had basically the same educational background. In most aspects, we were a group of peers.

After the meal, we were briefed on the upcoming building project. It had been prearranged that a few couples would share a word of testimony. The first husband and wife stood. They said that after a lot of prayer, they had decided to give five thousand dollars to the project. The second couple affirmed that they, too, believed very much in the project; they were going to sell their boat and give seven thousand dollars to the project. The third couple mentioned something about foregoing part of their family vacation, and giving several thousand dollars to the project. Then there was an embarrassing silence while everyone waited to see if someone else wanted to stand and make a pledge.

I can tell you that, though it was in my heart to be a part of that project, I had a very difficult time hearing the voice of my inner man that night; there was just too much external pressure. I certainly did not want to be seen as one giver who was not committed to the building project. I didn't want anyone thinking that I didn't manage my money well enough to have some left over to give. I didn't want anyone thinking that I was unwilling to sell my possessions in order to give to the project.

I have often thought about what would have happened if I had prayed and felt that God had said, "You are to give one hundred dollars." Would I have had the courage to stand up, after all my peers had pledged so much, and say with confidence and joy, "In obedience to God, my wife and I are going to give one hundred dollars"? In all honesty, I have to tell you that I would have had a hard time doing that. I would have been too embarrassed!

THE FOUR FEARS

You may say, in response to that situation, "Well, Dudley, that's your problem. You should be more secure than that."

I agree. But that's the whole point of manipulation, isn't it? It appeals to our fears and our insecurities.

In fact, I have discovered that certain hang-ups make us especially vulnerable to being manipulated. They all have to do with different fears that control fleshly men and women. They can be stated succinctly as follows: (1) the fear of punishment, (2) the fear of failure, (3) the fear of rejection, and (4) the fear of incompetence.

Those who fear punishment will always be trying to cover up or make up for their sins. They will fear exposure and do whatever it takes to keep from having their innermost being exposed. Deep down, they are terrified of what will happen if anyone—even God—found out what they are really like. Like disobedient children, they just know they are going to "get it."

But God gives them a solution to this fear in the new covenant. When we are in Christ, he says, we don't have to fear punishment. Once we repent and turn to Christ, our sins are forgiven and forgotten. They're gone. There's no punishment because, in God's eyes, there's no more sin.

People who are controlled by the fear of failure will spend most of their time trying to get ahead. Their insecurity may cause them to succeed in many projects, but they will never have the peace of God in their hearts. Their focus will be on doing the right things and believing the right doctrines, but they will always try to do these things on their own, not in dependence on God. They are doomed to failure.

God's answer to this fear is also found in the new covenant. He said he would put his law in our hearts and in our minds, causing us to know the will of God and giving us both the desire and the ability to do it. The new covenant focus is on living out of who we are in Christ rather than by what we do on our own.

The fear of rejection makes people vulnerable to applause, flattery, emotional blackmail, self-consciousness, and embarrassment. But God has solved this problem, too, in the new covenant. He has totally identified with the new-covenant people, receiving them as his own and giving himself totally to them. Their acceptance is based not on anything they do or don't do, but on something Jesus has already done. New-covenant people are fully and totally accepted by God through Jesus Christ. Once that reality is internalized, the fear of rejection loses its sting.

The fear of incompetence causes men and women to seek false credibility, to work feverishly for titles and degrees, to spend their lives jockeying for position at home, in business, and at church. But God has solved this problem also. He made it clear that in the new covenant our credibility will be based on his competence, not our own. Furthermore, we will not have to learn about God through oral tradition or intellectual acumen; he will reveal himself to our spirits.

WHY MANIPULATION IS HARMFUL

In the new covenant, God clearly rules out manipulation as the way to lead people and reach them with the gospel. Rather than use common fears and insecurities as tools to further his purposes, God offers solutions for those hang-ups. The obvious implication is that manipulation is out as a tool for those who minister his gospel of grace.

So why do ministries succumb to the temptation of manipulation? Could it be that we are succumbing to our own insecurities, closing ourselves to the workings of grace in our own lives?

After all, manipulation does work—up to a point—and it produces quick external results. Manipulative tools can coerce people into attending services, giving money, working hard, and serving long. The down side is that, in the end, ministers who manipulate are not furthering the purposes of the gospel. Instead of building up individuals and helping them grow, manipulation destroys them on the inside.

The problem with "bewitching tactics" is that, even when they bring the right external behavior, they tend to shrivel and frustrate the inner person.

When people are manipulated into giving an offering, for example, the desire does not come from within. As a result, the givers do not experience the joy and freedom that comes from obeying God. No wonder they are frustrated! They're experiencing the sacrifice without the reward, the pain without the gain. If the manipulation continues, they are likely to grow bitter and critical. Perhaps that's why so many people are critical of churches that need money or of ministries that seek contributions. It's not that they don't want to give. They are simply bitter and frustrated inside about being manipulated and frustrated on the inside.

MINISTRY WITHOUT MANIPULATION

How, then, do we minister without manipulation? We can take some clues from the fact that ministers are often compared to shepherds. And, as someone has so aptly said, "If you're going to raise sheep correctly, you must cooperate with sheep life." Jesus, in using the analogy of the shepherd and the sheep, gives us some facts about sheep life that will help us understand our role as undershepherds, working in ministry under the Good Shepherd's direction.

First, Jesus said, "My sheep hear my voice." If that's the case, they certainly don't need to focus on any other person's voice, including that of the minister. As a minister of the new covenant, therefore, it is my responsibility to encourage my flock to distinguish and listen to the voice they are already hearing—the voice of Jesus.

Several years ago, I was leading a discipleship group. During a time of testimony, I asked some of the group members how they were handling various situations in their lives. One of them reported eagerly, "When I run into a problem, I just ask myself what Dudley would say about it."

I'm sure that young man thought I would be pleased with his answer, but I was devastated. "Is this what I have done?" I thought. "Have I taught these people to think like I think? If so, I am a miserable failure as an undershepherd. My job is not to get them to think like me, but to get them to listen more closely to the voice of Jesus they are already hearing in their spirit."

"I'm honored that you consider me a good example of a Jesus follower," I told him. "So let me tell you what Dudley would think. Recognizing that Jesus talks to all his sheep, he would ask Jesus for wisdom."

Second, Jesus said, "My sheep follow me." What does that say to me as a minister? Simply that I don't have to force my flock to follow Jesus or trick them into following him. He is the Good Shepherd. He will lead them in paths of righteousness for his name's sake. He will make them to lie down in green pastures and lead them beside still waters (Ps 23).

My job as an undershepherd, a new-covenant minister, is not to push people toward certain behaviors, but only to operate consistently with the truths of the new covenant and to do all I can to help others be aware of those truths.

What is the gist of that new covenant? God wrote his law on my heart. He makes me to know and desire his ways. The cross is our victory; there, sin is forgiven, self is crucified, Satan is defeated, and Jesus is crowned Lord of everything. God, my heavenly Father, has totally identified with me. The law has been satisfied and has no further claim on me.

When these truths become more than theory in my life, I can incorporate them into my philosophy of ministry. Then I discover that my primary job is to help believers discover their own relationship with God and their own place in the new covenant.

THE TACTICS OF ENCOURAGEMENT

And how do I do that? Through encouragement.

The New Testament contains approximately thirty "reciprocal commands"—commandments that tell believers how to treat each other. "Admonish one another," "encourage one another," "bear one another's burdens," "be hospitable toward one another," "teach one another"—all of these instructions have encouragement at their core. All of them aim at building up the inner person. They are not so much behavior-oriented as spirit-oriented.

Let me suggest three primary ways of encouraging believers.

First, we are to remind one another of God's faithfulness. Whenever our focus shifts from human performance to divine faithfulness, faith increases and self-consciousness ceases. When all the world is screaming that it's time to panic, a focus on the faithfulness of God will bring peace in the midst of the storm.

One of the great benefits of Bible study is seeing the faithfulness of God throughout all generations and his commitment to us through Jesus Christ and the new covenant. All through the Old Testament, when the people of God are faced with difficult circumstances, they go back over their past history with God and glean encouragement by being reminded of his faithfulness in every situation. The hymns we sing, too, are wonderful "memory joggers" of the faithful ways God deals with his people.

Second, we are to join together in thankfulness. Thankfulness takes our eyes off ourselves and puts them on God, where they should be in the first place. It is very difficult to be bewitched if your total focus is on the goodness of God and what he is providing for you rather than on what you should be doing or what you have or haven't done. Maybe this is the reason Paul said in his Epistles, "Give thanks always for all things." Thankfulness automatically takes our focus off the natural physical and puts it on the reality of God's goodness.

Third, we are to "stimulate one another to love and good deeds, not forsaking our own assembling together... but encouraging one another." This is the climactic command of a wonderful passage—Hebrews 10:19-25. The entire Book of Hebrews, you remember, was written to help us know how to operate in the new covenant, as opposed to the old covenant. And all the wonderful truths of that Epistle are summed up in this brief passage. Its focus is on the cause-and-effect relationship of what God has done for us in Jesus Christ and how we are to live. Understanding the nature of this gift and this response really simplifies Christian living and Christian ministry.

At the beginning of the Hebrews passage, we are given two verses that start off with "since" and three that start off with "let us." "*Since*... we have confidence to enter the holy place by the blood of Jesus" (v. 19) and "*since* we have a great high priest over the house of God" (v. 21), three things should be as natural for us as breathing is to the living soul:

- First, "*Let us draw near*" (v. 22). That is, let us enjoy the intimacy with God that is provided by the blood of Jesus Christ and by his intercession for us as the "great high priest."
- Next, "*Let us hold fast the confession of our hope*" (v. 23). Why? Because he who promised is faithful. The high priest who is interceding for us will not fail.
- And finally, "*let us consider how to stimulate one another to love and good deeds*" (v. 24).

Notice that the word here is *stimulate*, not *manipulate*. To manipulate means to use some kind of external force to coerce a person into altering his behavior. To stimulate means that there is already life on the inside; it simply needs to be encouraged. To me, it's a picture of an ember that just needs someone to blow on it in order to burst into flame.

OBSTACLES AND OPPORTUNITIES

New-covenant ministers, essentially, can do only two things for others.

First, we can help remove obstacles that are keeping people from carrying out what is written in their hearts and in their minds. These obstacles can be fears, misconceptions, habits, strongholds. Through love and witness, a minister can help remove these barriers and open the way for faith to operate freely.

Second, we can help provide opportunities for God's people to do what they have already been programmed to do by their new birth.

Looking at ministry in light of these two tasks helps shed light on how best to minister without manipulation. It is not wrong, for example, for ministers to give us opportunities for service. Christians need to be challenged to do what is in their hearts to do—to believe, to serve, to give. Placing opportunities in front of others is not necessarily manipulation. Only when the inner person is sacrificed to external behavior does manipulation replace ministry.

Manipulation is *playing God.* That is a tiring and exasperating experience; you are just not equipped for it. If you fall into the habit of relying on manipulation in the service of ministry, your energy level will not hold out. In the long run, you cannot be successful. Ministry, on the other hand, is *following God,* immersing yourself in the reality of the gospel of grace and responding to his leadership as you lead others.

With all this in mind, let's call a halt to manipulative ministry. If you've been the victim of manipulation, forgive those who were involved, receive the truth that's liberating your soul now, and allow the new covenant to be internalized so you are no longer vulnerable to the manipulation of the flesh.

If you've been involved as a manipulator, ask forgiveness right now and receive a new assignment from the Lord. In place of manipulative ministry, you have the great opportunity, as a partner with the Holy Spirit in new covenant ministry, to encourage others to listen to the voice of the Shepherd and to follow him. And all the while, you have the wonderful privilege of following him as well.

PART FOUR

Grace and the Simple Life

O Lord, my heart is not proud, nor my eyes haughty;
Nor do I involve myself in great matters,
Or in things too difficult for me.
Surely I have composed and quieted my soul;
Like a weaned child rests against his mother,
My soul is like a weaned child within me.
Psalm 131:1-2

CHAPTER

18 The Scandal of Simplicity

DURING MY SEMINARY STUDIES, I was called as pastor for a little church in Fort Worth, Texas. Part of my work, of course, would involve counseling. I was very apprehensive about serving as a counselor to people with serious problems. After all, I was a young man and had little experience in counseling. So whenever people would set up an appointment to come by and talk about their serious problems, I would pray long and hard, asking God to give me wisdom.

I hadn't been at that church very long, however, when I discovered a strange phenomenon. Most of the time, the solution to my parishioners' problems would be obvious to me within a few moments of hearing their story. Often I would feel like a first grader who knows the answer to the teacher's question. Inside I would be holding my hand up, jumping up and down, and saying, "I know the answer! I know! I know!"

The counselee would pause. I would confidently share the solution to the problem. Then I would be shocked to find that the person would simply take up where he or she had left off and continue telling me how bad things really were.

I realize now, of course, that often those people needed someone to care about them and listen to them as much as they needed a solution, but I think there's another reason my parishioners didn't want to take my advice. Over my years in the ministry I've come to see that people really do not want simple solutions to complex problems. And that's because they've bought into the lie of complexity.

The longer I live, the more I believe that God is perfect simplicity. The closer things get to God's original intent, the simpler they will be. The more fallen humanity tampers with things, the more they move toward complexity. It was the recognition of this truth that caused Paul to write to the Christians at Corinth, "But I am afraid, lest as the serpent deceived Eve by his craftiness, your minds should be led astray from the simplicity and purity of devotion to Christ" (2 Cor 11:3).

Inevitably, however, the god of this world takes the simple things of God and moves them toward complexity. As a result, most people really have bought the lie that serious problems demand complicated solutions. The natural mind tends to be scandalized by simplicity.

A PARABLE FOR OUR PROBLEMS

A good illustration of the natural tendency to resist simple solutions is found the story of Naaman, the Syrian. I believe Naaman's tale is a good parable for all of humanity's problems.

First of all, Naaman had a problem that seemed to complicate his life immensely. In some ways, Naaman had it made. He was captain of the armies of Syria. Because of his position he enjoyed wealth, prestige, and prominence; he lived in luxury. But Naaman was a leper. Leprosy was considered by most cultures to be not only a physical disease, but also a curse from the gods.

Naaman's life, in other words, was a crazy combination of really good news and really bad news. In a sense, he had everything in life he could have asked for—but he was stymied by an "if only" that seemed to block his happiness.

Now, Naaman's "if only" was truly life-threatening. Some of ours are, too. But our problems don't have to be as bad as leprosy to keep us from enjoying the good things we do have. Think about it. Would your life be better "if only" you were a little taller, or "if only" you weren't so fat, or "if only" you your children were different or you had a better job or you lived in a better part of town?

Naaman's disease also predisposed him to shame and isolation and loneliness. In his day, leprosy was considered highly contagious, and lepers were usually separated from the public. And leprosy is a disfiguring disease; no doubt it filled him with self-disgust. Even if society didn't shun him, chances are that Naaman would want to hide.

Isolation and loneliness are among the most severe problems we modern humans seem to suffer, too. When we are conscious of our imperfections and our problems, we tend to isolate ourselves, even if others do not reject us.

Many of us suffer from a case of spiritual leprosy that keeps us from enjoying the relationships that we were designed to enjoy. Husbands and wives live in the same house and sleep in the same bed with a partner that they never really get to know. Parents spend eighteen years with children that they raised but never really got to know. Suburbanites attend neighborhood meetings and yet never get to know the people next door. Christians even go to church with fellow believers, yet never let down the barriers enough to get acquainted.

Now, isn't it strange that the human solution to this loneliness problem is to become more independent? The more complex our lives become, the more we want to "get away from it all"—and for most of us, that means getting away from other people as well. Some of us move from the city to the suburbs, then from the suburbs to the country. Some of us take off on wilderness vacations, trying desperately to simplify our lives by getting out to be alone. When are we going to realize that God made people to relate to other people—that only in relationships will we find the simple fulfillment of life?

NAAMAN SEEKS A SOLUTION

But back to Naaman. He has a big "if only" problem, one that stands in the way of his happiness and cuts him off from other people. In fact, his problems get so serious that he is willing to take an offensive solution.

Someone has accurately said that when our desperation factor exceeds our embarrassment factor, we are a candidate for grace. Well, Naaman finally qualified for grace. He was so tired of his leprosy that he was even willing to take a suggestion from his wife's handmaiden, who happened to be a Hebrew slave. She tells him of a prophet in Samaria named Elisha who could heal him of his leprosy.

What a slam in the face—having to receive advice from a little slave girl! But Naaman is desperate enough to try anything. He goes to his commander and asks for permission to go to Israel to see this man named Elisha. And the king gives him a letter to take to the king of Israel. The Syrian king is assuming that peers must relate to peers. Surely, he reasons, if any man in the land of Israel can help Naaman, it will be a man of importance.

How apropos. Some people will not receive the solution to their problem from one who is not in their admiration category.

I am always amused at the people in a church who seem to need "counsel" periodically—and will only take counsel from their senior paster. I wonder if what they really want is to be recognized by someone they deem important. It may not even be a conscious thought in their mind, but somehow they have concluded, "If significant people will give me time, I must be significant, too."

At any rate, Naaman goes to the king of Israel to ask for assistance. And when the king of Israel gets the letter, he tears his clothes. He knows he has no capability to bring healing to Naaman. And he fears that failing to help Naaman will make him an enemy of the powerful king of Syria.

Now, Elisha hears what has happened. He sends word to the

king of Israel, advising him to stop tearing his clothes and calm down. "Send the man to me. I can cure him of his leprosy," says Elisha.

OFFENDED BY A SIMPLE SOLUTION

So here's the picture. Naaman and his train of chariots drive up in front of Elisha's house. It's quite a scene—pomp and splendor and majesty. Naturally, the Syrian captain expects a big reception from this Israeli prophet. Instead, Elisha sends his aide out to give a message to Naaman. Here's how it goes:

"Is this Elisha's house?" Naaman inquires.

"Yes it is," the aide replies, "and Elisha said for me to give you a message. You are to go down to the River Jordan and dip seven times. Do that and you'll be clean."

"You're not Elisha?" Naaman demands.

"No," says Gehazi, the aide.

"And Elisha is not coming out to see me?" says Naaman.

"Ah, no sir, ah, he's busy. But he did tell me to tell you..."

"Am I not important enough for him to come out?"

"Well, sir, he told me to tell you..."

"I thought surely he would come out and say some complicated formula over me, lay his hand on me or something," protested Naaman.

"Well, he did tell me to tell you..."

"Does he not know that I am the captain of the armies of Syria?"

"Ah, yes sir, he does know that."

"Is he not going to come out and pray over me and do some religious exercise for me?"

"Ah, no sir. He said for me to tell you to go down to the River Jordan and dip seven times."

The simplicity of Elisha's message is very offensive to Naaman. He is a very important person; he wants an important person to deal with him. And the message itself is offensive to his mind. "How ridiculous. Dip seven times in a muddy river. What good would it do?"

Naaman is so angry that he is ready to go back home. But his own servants come to him and say, "If he had told you to do something complicated, would you have done it?" That question struck at the heart of Naaman's problem. Simplicity is offensive. When Naaman accepted the simple solution and in obedience dipped himself in the River Jordan, he was totally and miraculously healed. A complex problem was solved with the simplest of solutions. All that was required of Naaman was to swallow his pride and take the solution that was offered.

AN OFFENSE TO THE MIND

When I've noticed people are terribly disappointed by my offering a simple solution to their problem, I've often been tempted to give them a complicated one instead. I've thought of saying, "Go home and find a purple pail. Pour in two parts alcohol, one part bleach, and three parts vinegar. Place your right foot in the bucket and turn around four times clockwise while quoting the twenty-third Psalm. Then put your left foot in the bucket and turn counterclockwise while praying the Lord's Prayer. When you finish, lie in a prone position for forty minutes; when you get up, your problem will be solved." I really believe a lot of people would be more likely to follow that instruction than the simple instructions that will really solve their problems.

One day, after I had finished speaking at a particular meeting, a woman came up and told me, "I need to be slain in the Spirit." She had obviously seen people fall unconscious in certain ministry situations and thought that experience would solve her problems. I looked at her and said, as gently as I could, "Then why have you come to me? I'm not the Holy Spirit, and I can't slay you."

She hurriedly explained that she had much confusion in

her life, and that she had also severely injured her ankle only a few days before and needed healing in her body. She was certain that if she were "knocked out" in the Spirit, all of this would be fixed.

I simply said, "Why don't you tell Jesus where you hurt, then go home and take a nap."

That night the woman came back, running to me and telling me her story. "I realize," she said, "how ridiculous I was in trying to prescribe to God how he was supposed to fix me. I did exactly what you said. I told him about my need and went home and took a nap. When I awoke, not only had my confusion left, but now I am walking freely without pain in my ankle."

Now, I am not saying that one prayer and a nap will make all our problems go away. God knows what we need and answers our prayers on his own timetable. But I do think it's important to recognize that God will not be entrapped in our schemes to make life complicated. He holds on to simplicity. And he is not afraid to offend our minds with the simplicity of his answers.

Sometimes, in fact, it seems that God goes out of his way to offend our minds. He does it for a reason. Ever since the first humans ate from the Tree of the Knowledge of Good and Evil, humankind has wanted to understand everything—to have life categorized, systemized, and codified. But since God wants us living by the Tree of Life and not the Tree of the Knowledge of Good and Evil, he is constantly offending our minds. He wants us to live by trusting him—not by having things under control.

THE ULTIMATE OFFENSE

In fact, when God performed his ultimate act of redemption and healing for a lonely, self-conscious, and sinful human race—sending his Son to earth—he did it in a way that a lot of humans just couldn't swallow.

Think about it. Jesus' being born to a virgin offended the minds of "nice people" in his hometown. So did the circumstances of his birth. He was born in a barn, remember. And it was probably not a nice little cozy stable like we see at Christmas time, where all the straw is clean and the animals are calm, but a dirty, stinking barn. What a place for a king to be born!

This king was raised in the countryside of Galilee and probably spoke with a country accent. What an offense! Surely if God were going to send someone to save the world, he wouldn't do it this way.

He waited thirty years before he even got started on a ministry. Does that make sense? Since he was God, surely he knew his time was limited. Why not get started sooner? When he finally did get started, he didn't start in the population center of the country, but out in the countryside. He called common men to help him; he spoke to the common people. And he refused to play to the crowds. In fact, whenever the multitudes became large, he would walk off and leave them.

On one occasion, when the crowds were getting large, Jesus thinned them out by telling them that from now on, if anyone wanted to follow him, they would have to eat his flesh and drink his blood!

It worked. The multitudes began leaving by the droves. Finally, he looked at his disciples and said, "Will you, too, leave?" And they must have looked a little grossed out as they told him, in essence, "We would, except you're the only one who has the words of life."

Jesus offended everybody's minds, including those of disciples. They were willing to walk through the offense because of the life they found in him. But they must have felt relieved when Jesus explained that he was talking about spiritual realities, not physical flcsh and blood.

The relief didn't last long, however. The disciples' minds were offended again and again as Jesus tried to explain to them how God's redemptive plan would unfold. The Son of

God suffering on a cross... and then rising from the dead? It just didn't make sense.

It was only much later that they began to understand: From an eternal perspective, Jesus' redemptive death and resurrection makes the best kind of sense possible.

God has been demonstrating from the very beginning that he refuses to fit into our neat little categories. Why, then, do we continue to require God to do things that fit into the understanding of our natural mind? I love the succinct simplicity of the gospel writer, Mark, who summarizes the ministry of Jesus in a single paragraph: "And after John had been taken into custody, Jesus came into Galilee, preaching the gospel of God, and saying, the time is fulfilled and the kingdom of God is at hand; repent and believe in the gospel" (Mk 1:14-15).

Those are the simple essentials of salvation: repent and believe. That's enough. Nothing more needs to be said.

The internal conflicts we experience are because we have believed a lie and are living in deception. But Jesus made it abundantly clear that knowing the truth will make us free. The only reason we are not free is that somehow, in some area, we have not embraced the truth.

Now, I don't want to be condemning or misleading here. Simple is not the same thing as simplistic—and simple certainly isn't the same thing as easy. In fact, some of the simplest acts in the world are the hardest to do. The simple solution of embracing the truth about ourselves and the world, repenting of our lies and self-deception, and trusting ourselves to God's saving mercy may indeed involve some pain and struggle on our part. It's hard to give up our self-will. It's hard to let go of the lies we hide behind. To embrace God's simple solution, we may well need the help of others, just as Naaman needed Elisha's help. And it might take time.

But once we reach the point that we can see it and embrace it, the ultimate solution to our problems shines through all the seeming complexities of our lives with beautiful simplicity.

That's the reason the gospel can be preached anywhere, to any culture, at any time. Any human being can repent and believe. Anyone can know the truth, reject the deception, embrace the truth, and experience the liberty of God.

And it's just as simple as that.

CHAPTER

19 Simplicity as a Perspective

A FEW YEARS AGO, a man from the West coast dropped by our office to visit. He said he was familiar with our ministry and had seen me a few times on television. He had ordered some tapes and listened to messages I had given, and he had a question.

"You seem to have found something of the secret of resting and being at peace. So, how do you do it? What is the secret of living without turmoil? Talking to you is like sitting by still waters."

I laughed and told him that might not be a compliment; after all, a mud puddle is still water. But then, in seeking to answer his question, I was called to verbalize succinctly something I had never really tried to verbalize before.

I heard myself saying to him something like this. "By temperament, I am not an aggressive or excitable person. But all my life, I was well acquainted with inner strife and anxiety. From an early age, I'd had a desire to know God and follow his ways. I spent many years seeking to discover all his principles and to live by them. I wanted to become an expert in understanding the ways of God.

"I reached a point, however, when the principles I was discovering turned out to be too many, and I realized I just did not have the mental capacity to decipher the multifaceted wisdom of Almighty God. It was during that time that I had a brief glimpse of God himself that completely overturned my perception of reality and taught me the secret of internal rest.

"I can't really say it was a vision, for I don't remember actually seeing anything, but somehow I was given an acute awareness of who God really is. I saw him with the eyes of my spirit, and I discovered was that *he is very big and very good.* Ever since that day, my perspective has changed. I've been able to keep my focus simple. And when I do that, I am able to be at peace."

"Very big and very good." What poor words to describe what I really saw! To say that God is big is the greatest understatement that could ever be made. To say that he is good does not begin to describe the character of our Father. But the point is: I began to be free of inner turmoil not when I focused on the complexity of God's principles, but when I perceived the awesomely simple truth of who he is. And that change of perspective dramatically changed the way I looked at everything else in my life.

WHY COMPLICATE THINGS?

Have you noticed that some people just see things in a complicated fashion? A few years ago, I made plans to travel to Mexico with a group of men for a hunting retreat. We would spend the morning in fellowship and Bible study, and in the afternoon we would go on a hunting expedition.

One of the young men on this trip had assumed the responsibility of keeping the expedition of our group organized. He was one of those people who thought in such detail that his life was always complicated.

I remember one afternoon he was all in a dither over our schedule. Remember, we were in Mexico, where everything is laid-back and nobody is in a hurry for anything. And all we were going to do was get some ice, put it in a cooler, put in some water and cold drinks, drive out to a field, hunt for a little while, and come back. Our schedule couldn't be complicated. And yet Jack made it an issue of monumental proportion.

He gathered the whole group of men around and said, "Men, we have to make a decision now. It's two o'clock in the afternoon, and we have to know what kind of schedule we are going to operate on. Now, there are several options. We can either go get the ice now and bring it back and put the drinks on it and then go hunting, or we can take the drinks with us and stop by and pick up the ice on the way and go hunting then. Now, which way do you think would be the most advantageous?"

All the men sat around in stunned silence. Nobody could believe what he was hearing. Finally, we all broke into laughter. "Who cares?" someone said. "Let's just do it."

Some people just seem to see life through complex glasses. Life to them is a matrix of decisions, agendas, and schedules. Everything must be figured out, and every decision is major. To fail in a small decision causes as much disruption as failure in the big ones.

Other people seem to have found simplified glasses. They can look at the most complicated situation, see through all the complexities, and cut to the heart of the situation. They seem to have internalized the advice given by a friend: "Don't sweat the small stuff... and remember, it's *all* small stuff."

That second perspective, I'm convinced, is the key to inner serenity.

Now, I'm not saying that details are unimportant. I'm certainly not saying we shouldn't rely on schedules or plans; trying to live on the spur of the moment can be even more complicated than planning out every minute. I'm talking about the way we look at our lives—the overall perspective we bring to the way we live. In all the details of our lives, we always have the choice to focus on the simple reality of who is really in charge. And that focus us what keeps us from drowning in complexity.

LEARNING FROM ASAPH

One of the most graphic pictures of a man who has allowed his life to get mired in complexity is found in Psalm 73. Asaph, traditionally considered the writer of this psalm, was also the praise leader for Israel. Here was a man who had every opportunity to have life in its proper perspective. And yet something had gone awry; life had become too complicated to enjoy. I think that looking at this psalm can give us some clues to maintaining a simple perspective.

Listen to Asaph's story.

Surely God is good to Israel,
  to those who are pure in heart!
But as for me, my feet came close to stumbling...
  I was envious of the arrogant,
as I saw the prosperity of the wicked.
  For there are no pains in their death....
They are not in trouble as other men....
Surely in vain I have kept my heart pure,
  and washed my hands in innocence;
for I have been stricken all day long,
  and chastened every morning....

When I pondered to understand this,
  it was troublesome in my sight
until I came into the sanctuary of God;
  then I perceived their end.

The first thing we learn from Asaph is our lives get complicated when our perspective is limited. And our perspective will always be limited if it does not include revelation from God.

The particular complication in Asaph's life was the fact that the cause-and-effect principle he had always believed to be true just didn't seem to be working. Asaph knew, for instance, that God is good to those who are pure in heart and that God punishes the wicked. To Asaph, that was a given—the way things were set up. But when Asaph looked around him, he discovered things were not working out according to that principle. The wicked seemed to be prospering, and Asaph's own efforts at keeping himself holy just didn't seem to be paying off. This confused him.

Any time you depend on a principle without the added perspective of revelation, you're on the road to complexity. Obviously, there is great truth to the principle that there is a cause to every effect. And much wisdom can be gained by knowing what causes bring certain effects. But the human mind is too small to decipher and delineate all the cause-and-effect relationships that are built into this universe.

When life depends on knowing all the principles relating to our circumstances, it inevitably becomes very complicated. We would have to carry around a fifteen-pound notebook just to remind us of all the principles we are to follow—and we would still be in danger of slipping up somewhere. Say that you are told that there are eleven ways a man is supposed to treat his wife if he is going to be a good husband... I am in a real mess if I can only remember nine. Or there are fourteen ways to solve a financial crisis.... And what if I can only remember seven? If there are fifteen ways to deliver an addict, six steps to being filled with the Spirit... how can I possibly keep track?

Please don't misunderstand. Learning principles can be very helpful. It would be foolish to live in God's ordered world without a sound basic knowledge of how things are set up. But no one will ever gain enough insight to live successfully apart from revelation by Jesus himself. We must have an encounter with something beyond the rational mind in order to keep from being overwhelmed.

Asaph's testimony fits us all. "When I pondered to understand this, it was troublesome in my sight."

DON'T JUDGE BY THE APPARENT

You're familiar with the story of Job. Job was a man whom God himself declared to be righteous, and yet he endured one terrible circumstance after another. Job's friends came to help

Job in his affliction. And basically, those friends were dealing with him on the basis of cause and effect. They were saying things like this:

"Job, you understand that God blesses the good and curses the wicked."

"Yes," Job said, "I understand that."

"You understand, Job, that it would be unjust for God to justify the wicked and curse the righteous."

"Yes, that would seem to be the case," said Job.

"Well, Job, we want to help you now, and we would like for you to think through this situation you're in. Would you say you are being blessed or cursed at this moment?"

Job considers that he has lost all his family, he's lost all his wealth, his own body is covered with sores, and his wife is standing over in the corner of the kitchen telling him to curse God and die.

He replies, "It appears that I'm not being blessed."

"That's exactly right," Job's friends say, "so what conclusion should we come to?"

"But I'm righteous," says Job.

His friends sigh at his imperceptiveness. "Job, Job, Job," they say. "God gives good things to those who do right; he gives bad things to those who do wrong. Are you getting good things or bad things, Job?"

"I know what you're saying," Job says. "I know it appears that I am being cursed because of my unrighteousness. But I tell you, I have not disobeyed God."

If you'll remember the end of the story, God is not very pleased with the counsel of Job's three friends. It is never enough to judge things simply by our understanding of cause and effect principles.

So much worldly understanding is based on the premise that the present can be explained in terms of the past. In fact, we have a whole generation of people who are preoccupied with their personal past. Everything that is wrong in their life must have been caused by something when they were younger.

"I'm a failure because my father didn't love me properly." "I'm having trouble with my wife because my mother never totally released me." "I can't relate to God as a father because my earthly father was not perfect."

Now, there is some truth in the fact that unresolved conflicts in the past can affect us in the present. But a preoccupation with the past will paralyze us. In order to understand and solve our problems, we need more than just a casual observation of cause and effect. We need a change of perspective that assures us God is bigger than cause and effect—that he's completely in charge of what's going on in the universe and in our lives.

GOD IS IN CHARGE

Notice when Asaph got help.

"When I came into the sanctuary of God, then I perceived their end."

Life becomes simple when one is able to see from the divine perspective. And the thing one sees from the divine perspective is that God himself is absolutely sovereign.

Now please, don't allow your mind to run off into all the possible objections. God's sovereignty is something that can be perceived, but cannot be adequately explained. When we do try to explain it, we usually end up with some kind of distorted fatalism—just as when we try to explain human responsibility, we end up crediting ourselves with more responsibility than we really have.

God is in charge. Asaph said, in essence, "When I came into the presence of God, I discovered that he was so much in charge that I could just sit back and let him be God." If you could resist the urge to try and understand this and just enjoy it for a little while, you would be forever different.

All of us have a curiosity about what makes things tick. When I was a little boy, two of my playmates were my niece and my female cousin, and they often wanted to play with dolls. I was intrigued by those dolls that could talk. I was always begging the girls to let me take them apart to find out what made them talk. They were afraid—justifiably—that if I pulled the dolls' heads off to find out how they worked, the dolls would be ruined. So they never let me pursue my investigations. And that was one reason I didn't really like playing with the dolls. I was too preoccupied with finding out how they worked just to relax and enjoy them.

I felt the same way when my family's first television was brought into our house. I was about six years old, and I really wanted to know what made that thing work. I would go out in the yard and look at the antenna that had been erected beside our home. How did those pictures come through the air, go down that antennae, and come out in that box? It was an intriguing phenomenon. When the television needed repair, I would stand with the repairman and ask him questions all the time he was working, trying to understand how that television worked. I never got any satisfactory answers.

In this case, however, I finally made a monumental decision. "If I never understand how it works, I'm still going to enjoy it."

There are many things in life that are beyond our understanding but can still be enjoyed. We take a big step toward inner peace when we accept that reality.

Maybe you heard about the three men who were discussing the most amazing inventions of all times. One of them said he believed it was the television.

"It's amazing, when you think of it," he marveled. "How in the world can pictures thousands of miles away be transmitted through thin air and picked up in a box—at essentially the same time they are being produced in the studio? It's miraculous."

The second man's opinion was that the greatest invention was the microwave oven. "How do things cook without even getting hot on the outside? Now *that's* miraculous."

The third man then offered his opinion. "The most amazing invention ever," he said, "is a thermos bottle."

"A thermos bottle?" the others questioned. "What's so amazing about a thermos bottle? All it does is keep hot things hot and cold things cold."

"I know," said the third man. "But how does it know?"

We don't really need to understand how a television, a microwave, or even a thermos bottle work in order to enjoy them. Once you've internalized that reality, your life will become a lot less complicated.

The wonderful truth of perception is that, once you've seen in your spirit the reality of the sovereignty of God, your inner person can rest.

THE VIEW FROM THE SANCTUARY

What did Asaph see when he "came to the sanctuary of God" and adopted the divine perspective? Here's what he says: "I am continually with thee; thou has taken hold of my right hand. With thy counsel thou wilt guide me, and afterward receive me to glory" (Ps 73:23-24). This little confession outlines the vision of God that can rescue us from complexity and keep our hearts at peace:

God Is There. First, Asaph saw what every believer sees when he truly perceives the divine perspective. "I am continually with Thee."

In the complexity of the apparent, we are often made to believe that God has deserted us. We think he withdraws his presence because of our sin or because of our lack of sensitivity or whatever. But God has promised, "I will never desert you, nor will I ever forsake you" (Heb 13:5). In fact, he sent his Holy Spirit to live inside us so we can always live in the presence of God.

For the New Testament believer, life is not divided up into those times when God is present and those when he is absent; there is no time when God is not there. In the new covenant, God's Spirit and the human spirit have become one. (See

1 Corinthians 6:17.) We continually live in God's presence, and the Holy Spirit lives in us, making Jesus real to us. We don't have to go anywhere, do anything, or use any secret formula to be with God.

Separation is an illusion created by the Enemy to cause the New Testament believer to live in complexity. If we fall for the lie that something has separated us from God, we will spend all our time and energy trying to get back into his presence. What a waste! Trying to get back into God's presence is as foolish as trying to get into a room where you're already standing! It is when God opens our eyes, as he did for Asaph, and allows us to see that we are continually with him, that we cease from striving and begin to discover the secret of inner peace.

God Is Faithful. Second, Asaph saw God's eternal commitment to him: "Thou hast taken hold of my right hand."

Notice that Asaph didn't say he was holding onto God's hand—in Asaph's word picture, God does the holding. The proper view of sovereignty makes it clear: It is God's faithfulness in keeping his covenant with us that causes our response of worship and obedience.

When we see things from the proper perspective, the focus is on *God's* commitment to *us.* If we shift our view and focus instead on *our* commitment to *God,* we will find ourselves striving, for we humans simply do not have the capacity to be committed enough. But when we keep our eyes on God's faithfulness, our faith automatically increases.

Paul enunciated this great revelation like this: "If we died with him, we shall also live with him; if we endure, we shall also reign with him; If we deny him, he also will deny us; if we are faithless, he remains faithful, for he cannot deny himself" (2 Tm 2:11-13).

God Will Guide. But Asaph is not through with his new perceptions. "With thy counsel thou wilt guide me," he adds, "and afterward receive me to glory" (v. 24).

Not only did Asaph see that he was continuing in God's

presence and that God's commitment to him was ongoing; he also discovered what God was intending to do for him—to counsel him and guide him in all his paths, and ultimately take him to glory.

Some time ago, I became somewhat intimidated by all the visions and plans that I heard my fellow ministers enunciating. Many were describing all the great visions they had for the wonderful ministries they were going to be embarking in. They were talking about building large complexes, producing big-time television broadcasts, conducting huge crusades.

As I listened to them share their assignments, calls, commissions, and visions, I began to question whether or not I had an adequate vision. So I asked the Lord to take me back to my original call and commission. It was a wonderful experience to go back in time and hear that same voice and message I had heard many years earlier. I became newly aware that when God called me he did not spell out all the specifics. He did not tell me that I would spend my life always as a missionary; neither did he tell me that I would always be a pastor or an evangelist. What he said was "Follow me."

Now, I am not making light of the specific assignments God gives to individuals. He does that. But first, before those specifics assignments are made, he issues the simple call to follow. Our lives become immensely simpler and less stressed when we obey.

A few years ago I had the privilege of speaking at a large conference with several very prominent spiritual leaders. One night after the sessions, I was standing on the platform, chatting with some conference participants, when an old friend from college days spotted me.

He looked at me incredulously and asked, "How did you get on this platform?"

I said, "Well, I just walked up those steps over there."

He laughed politely, but then he persisted: "You know what I mean. How did you get up here with all these important people?"

I responded in honesty. "I don't know. It never was an issue. I can honestly say I never sat down and planned to be here. It was never part of my design; it was not even a desire in my heart. I have just been seeking to follow Jesus, and sometimes following him leads across certain platforms. Other times, it leads to quiet places. Sometimes it leads to obscurity. But the issue, always, is following him."

I've discovered, in fact, that if my first focus is not on following Jesus, my visions of projects and plans can be dangerous to me. I'm likely to get involved in work that drains my spirit and burns me out, work that does little to further God's kingdom.

God is my guide. He is my counsel. He has me by the right hand. He is so much in charge of my life, that he will even teach me how to pray when I don't know how to pray: "And in the same way the Spirit also helps our weakness; for we do not know how to pray as we should, but the Spirit himself intercedes for us with groanings too deep for words; and he who searches the hearts knows what the mind of the Spirit is, because he intercedes for the saints according to the will of God" (Rom 8:26-27).

How can I get my life in such a dither when God is so committed to guiding me that when I don't know how to pray, he prays for me? And it's not just a matter of prayer. When I don't know how to be holy, he is there. When I don't know how to be strong, his strength is mine. When I don't have the wisdom to solve a problem, his wisdom is mine.

HOW TO ENJOY LIFE MORE

God is very big and very good. He is in charge of the universe. And we can rely on his constant presence, his faithfulness, his guidance.

God, in other words, is sovereign. And seeing life from that perspective simplifies life immensely.

The sovereignty of God should never be a theological

premise that is discussed in the confines of the church. It is the liberating reality of who God is and how we relate to him. Perceiving God as sovereign does not lead us into passivity or irresponsibility. Instead, it causes us to become quiet on the inside so we can hear the voice of God directing us to be involved where God assigns us.

To those who have not seen this revelation of his sovereignty, life seems, by necessity, complicated. The devil looms bigger than he should be; daily decisions are too imposing. Success and failure ride too heavily on our shoulders.

If you haven't seen how big and how good God is, stop what you're doing and seek his face. Life is too short for you to spend it troubled by what you're pondering. Life is too short to live in complexity.

As I sat in my office that day, seeking to explain to my visitor how I had learned the secret of inner rest, I closed my brief synopsis with this statement: "I can't explain it, but I'm absolutely sure of this. When I get to heaven and see things as they really are, I know I'm going to snap my fingers and say, 'Shoot! If I had known God was this much in charge, I would have worried a whole lot less and enjoyed life a whole lot more!'"

CHAPTER

20 Simplified Sanctification

I HAD BEEN ASKED BY A GROUP of pastors to lead a conference on spiritual awakening. They had also requested that I invite someone to lead the praise and worship. I immediately called a friend who had served with me at a previous meeting and had done an excellent job. He indicated that he would check his schedule and get back with me soon. In a few days, I received his letter. It read something like this:

> Dear Dudley,
>
> Thank you so much for your invitation to lead the praise and worship at the upcoming conference. However, the last time I was in such a conference I learned so many truths about how to live a holy life, and I have not yet incorporated all those things into my life. I don't want to learn any more truth until I have put to work and perfected what I already know.

At first my thoughts were, "How admirable. Here is a man who is committed to putting everything he learns to work in his life." But the more I thought about what he had said, the more I realized that I, too, had some of those same feelings—and they weren't necessarily admirable. They just came from feeling overwhelmed and inadequate: "If I'm responsible for everything I know, then please don't tell me any more. I've got too much responsibility already."

That sounds a lot like the children of Israel when they had seen the majestic glory of God come down on Mount Sinai and shake the mountain. They said, in essence, "Please don't do that any more. We don't ever want to see that much revelation again. Just let Moses get the word and give it to us. That will be enough." (See Hebrews 12:18-20.)

Sanctification—the process of becoming holy—seems so hard when we think of it in terms of accumulating information and bringing my life in line with the principles, laws, and regulations of some perceived standard of holiness. But does sanctification really have to be that hard, that complicated?

Jesus is our model of a sanctified life, and his was certainly not a life of complexity. Remember, he was not just modeling a life for the Jewish culture of the first century but expressing the epitome of life for all people in every age. His summation of the sanctified life is found in these words, "I do what I see my Father do, and I say what I hear my Father say." (See John 5:19; 12:49.)

In other words, Jesus was saying that the process of becoming holy consists of hearing, seeing, and responding. He expanded on that simple formula in his parable of the sower and the seed.

You know the story. Jesus told about a man who scattered seed on different kinds of soil—and the condition of the soil directly affected the way the seeds grew.

The first soil was so hard and packed that the seed could not penetrate; it simply lay on the surface and was eaten by birds.

Another kind of soil was rocky and shallow. The seed sown in it germinated and sprang up quickly, but was unable to send down deep roots. When the sun grew hot, the plant shriveled and died.

In the third kind of soil, seed sprouted and grew, only to be choked out by thorns that came up around it.

But then there was the good soil. Seed planted in it sprouted and grew and produced a bountiful crop.

RECEIVING THE SEED

Through this parable Jesus was explaining to his disciples some things about the simplicity of becoming holy. And the first point he stressed was that sanctification is a simple as receiving a seed and not rejecting it.

The analogy of this parable is that a seed is powerful—and it has within it the capability of reproducing its parent. The Word of God is a living thing, and it, too, it has the capability of reproducing *its* parent, the character of God. Once the seed is received, it does all the work. All the soil has to do is remain receptive.

It is absolutely essential that we refuse to define the Word of God in terms of some theological premise or some written statement. The Bible makes it very clear that the Word of God is a much more vital reality. "The word of God is living and active and sharper than any two-edged sword" (Heb 4:12). Jesus said, "The words I have spoken to you are spirit and are life" (Jn 6:63).

James, in his Epistle, says that it was the Word that caused us to be born again (Jas 1:18). He goes on to say that receiving the word will save our souls. He, too, uses the planting analogy to show the continual reception of the living truth of God will save our thinking, feeling, and choosing. It will preserve, cleanse, and perfect our very souls. Listen to the testimony of James.

> Therefore putting aside all filthiness and all that remains of wickedness, in humility receive the word *implanted*, which is able to save your souls. But prove yourselves doers of the word, and not merely hearers who delude themselves. For if anyone is a hearer of the word and not a doer, he is like a man who looks at his natural face in a mirror; for once he has looked at himself and gone away, he has immediately forgotten what kind of person he was. But one who looks intently at the perfect law, the law of liberty, and abides by

it, not having become a forgetful hearer but an effectual doer, this man shall be blessed in what he does.

James 1:21-25, emphasis mine

In the parable, the word translated "seed" is the word from which we get our word *sperm*—and the same basic relationship is at work in that image. A woman receives sperm from her husband, and, from that point on, the sperm does the rest of the work of conception, swimming to unite with the egg. Conception takes place and, ultimately, children are produced. God is saying to us that holy living comes as simply, naturally, and miraculously as conceiving children. Our job is to receive the living Word; it then takes over the work of "conceiving" holiness in our hearts.

The critical first issue is to receive the Word. If the Word is not received, it will be snatched away by the Enemy. Once it is received and internalized, God sees to it that growth happens: "For whoever has, to him shall more be given; and whoever does not have, even what he has shall be taken away from him" (Mk 4:25). When revelation is received, more will be given. But when revelation is rejected, even that which has been given shall be taken away.

That is why no person will ever be able to accuse God of not giving him or her a chance. For the Word of God has gone out into all the earth, and everyone has received some revelation. When a person responds to that, God will see to it that he or she gets more, until enough revelation has been received for that person not only to be saved, but to be fully redeemed.

The other side of that coin, however, is that when we reject revelation, we are responsible not only for the revelation we reject, but all that we could have received had we responded to the initial revelation. The person who rejects a little revelation, thus stopping the flow, will be held accountable for all that he or she could have had. It is dangerous and deadly not to receive the Word of God.

ENEMIES OF GROWTH

Once the Word has been received, two primary enemies will try to stop its production.

First is *persecution*. In his parable Jesus explained that the sun that scorched the plant represented the persecution that inevitably comes to one who receives the Word. Make no mistake about it, there will be persecution. People with little minds will be offended by the true Word of God, for that Word is so big and so comprehensive that it cannot be contained in the little boxes that little minds try to put it in.

Human tradition will persecute the Word of God. Jesus spent his whole life as the living Word of God, being accused and persecuted by those who knew the Scriptures but refused to receive the Word. It seems that human beings are determined to live in their own comfort zones, and they will give to their traditions the authority that should only be given to revelation from God.

Fear of where truth might lead also causes persecution of those who receive the Word. I could not believe my ears one day as I listened to a speaker explain to his audience that no one should ever be encouraged to believe that God heals people physically today. His reasoning was this: "Think of those poor people who go in faith expecting God to heal, but when they pray their prayer is not answered as they expect, and they are disappointed. To prevent this kind of disappointment, let's not encourage anyone that God ever heals."

In order to prevent people from being disappointed, let's not allow them to have any hope? Talk about a self-fulfilling prophecy! That kind of mentality will never be able to receive the Word of God.

The second enemy that tries to prevent the seed from producing is the enemy of *complication*—represented in the parable by the choking thorns that crowded out the growing grain. Jesus defined complication in three phrases: the "worries of the world," the "deceitfulness of riches," and "desires for other things" (Mk 4:19).

The worries of this world will always fight against the truth that God is in control. As we mentioned in chapter 19, when we see that God has us by the right hand, we can hold to that word, regardless of our apparent circumstances. But you can be sure that troubles or tragedies will always be nipping at our heels, tempting us to give way to worry instead of trusting the sovereign God.

The deceitfulness of riches struggles against God's promise of security, significance, and pleasure. Material wealth sends out the seductive lie that it can make us secure, significant, and happy. But God's Word states unequivocally that these things are to be found only in a relationship with him.

Malachi speaks directly to this issue in the Old Testament. He advises that instead of spending our lives trying to accumulate riches, we should concentrate on giving. Malachi says that if we will give the way God has instructed us to give, three things will happen: "Bring the whole tithe into the storehouse ... and test me now in this," says the Lord of hosts, "if I will not open for you the windows of heaven, and pour out for you a blessing until it overflows. Then I will rebuke the devourer for you, so that it may not destroy the fruits of the ground.... And all the nations will call you blessed" (Mal 3:10-12).

Do you see what Malachi is saying? If we trust in the Word of God, we will have all that we need for our own pleasure—and more—"blessing until it overflows." We will have security, because God has "rebuked the devourer" to prevent the Enemy from taking away those things that God has given us. And we will have significance; the nations will call us blessed because of our relationship with God.

God, not riches, is the reliable source of pleasure, security, and significance. Money lies when it claims to be able to provide these needs. The fact is, if we have not received the promise of God's Word, we will most likely be deceived by the lies of riches.

The third aspect of complication is "the desire for other things." Jesus spoke to that issue very directly in Matthew 6:33: "Seek first [God's] kingdom and his righteousness; and all these things shall be added to you."

God has made the personal promise to us that, if we keep our focus on the kingdom of God, every "thing" we need will be given to us by him. It is our responsibility to seek the kingdom; it is his responsibility to provide the things. However, if this Word is not internalized, we will spend our lives seeking things, accumulating things, and then protecting those things.

I find it amusing to watch a lot of today's "successful" people. They have made a lot of money and bought themselves many things, and as a result they have turned into nothing more than glorified maintenance men. They no longer have time for their spouses, their children, their friends, or their neighbors because they must spend too much time maintaining their things. Many minimum-wage workers lead simpler, more fulfilling lives than many millionaires, simply because they don't have to maintain so many things.

I recently spent a fascinating couple of hours with a building contractor who taught me about the changing trends in home building. It seems that changes in culture changes the size of certain rooms. For instance, front porches went out of style in most areas several years ago—in the days of air conditioning, people just don't sit out on the porch. Parlors or "living rooms" are not very popular today; people prefer the less formal dens and family rooms. "And do you know what room continues to increase in size with every generation?" my contractor friend asked. "The closet."

I'm sure he's right. Some Americans have gone from a few clothes hanging on the back of the bedroom door to walk-in closets—even drive-in closets. One man was showing me his new home. It was lovely. "But let me show you my special room," he said. Then led me to his personal closet. It was larger than my whole bedroom and was filled with dozens of suits and scores of shoes. He would have to be a centipede to ever wear all those shoes!

So many of us have bought into that little bumper-sticker slogan: "Life is a game, and he who dies with the most toys... wins!" The word of Scripture on that attitude is simple and unequivocal: It's a lie!

DON'T SCRATCH UP THE SEED

So how complicated is sanctification so far? As complicated as receiving the Word and refusing to allow it to be distorted by persecution or complexity. But there is another temptation: scratching up the seed. Sanctification is simple, but it is also mysterious, and we easily fall into the trap of second-guessing the process.

Jesus tells another parable about seeds. It depicts a man who sows seed on the ground and then goes to bed. He gets up the next morning and discovers that nothing has happened. He goes to bed again. The next morning... still nothing. But then one morning, he goes out and he finds something *has* happened: "the seed sprouts up and grows—how, he himself does not know." I love that phrase, "He himself does not know how." Something simple and miraculous has happened, but the man has no explanation as to how he arrived at this point.

This is the mystery of sanctification. The seed does the work. But the great temptation is to grow impatient and scratch it up when it doesn't produce on our time schedule.

When my daughter was about ten years old, she wanted to plant a garden. I thought it would be a wonderful educational opportunity for father and daughter to garden together and learn some of the basic truths of agriculture. And having grown up on a farm, I thought I knew enough to be an adequate instructor.

We decided to grow tomatoes and potatoes—one crop that grows above the ground and one that grows below. This would give us a full range of reference in our agricultural education. We had a wonderful time cutting up the potatoes, and I enjoyed explaining to my daughter how the eyes on the potato are really the seed; the eyes sprout and grow into plants.

Once we got all the eyes prepared, we planted them about four inches into the earth. As we were planting them, I told my daughter, "It is very important not to become impatient and begin scratching around in the dirt, looking for the sprouts. If you do, you will break off the sprout and ruin the plant. Just wait," I assured her. "The plants will come up..."

Sure enough, several days after the potatoes were planted, I saw her out looking longingly at the ground. Nothing there but black dirt—not a sign of life. I could tell she was beginning to doubt that our potato crop was really going to produce.

A week passed. No potato plants. And I began to worry a little myself. I began to question my own agricultural knowledge. Maybe I had planted them upside down and they were headed toward China. No, no, no. What could be the problem? Maybe the ground was too wet. Maybe I didn't cut the eyes off right.

So, one day after work I decided to go out and check on the potatoes. I got down on my knees in the garden and began scratching tenderly to try to determine what was causing the delay. Sure enough, I had not scratched a half inch beneath the surface when I broke off the young sprout of the plant. And just as I did, I heard the back door open and the sound of my daughter's voice: "Dad, are you scratching up our potatoes?"

I was guilty. My impatience had led to the destruction of a potato plant.

Sanctification does take time. The reception can be instant, but the sprouting, the growth, and the complete fruit take a while. Jesus said it this way. "First the blade, then the head, then the mature grain in the head" (Mk 4:28). We have to be willing for the Word of God to grow.

One night as my wife and I were walking in the neighborhood, Betsy said something very startling.

"I don't think I believe something I'm hearing you preach," she said. "I hear you saying that I'm as valuable as Jesus and am treated by God the same way he treats Jesus. You're saying that my worth is not tied to my performance in anyway, that I am already a new creation in Christ. I don't think I believe that."

I said, "You mean you think that is a lie? Or are you saying you haven't seen the fruit of that in your life yet?"

"I must not believe it, or I would be different," she replied.

Now, Betsy's attitude is very common with all of us. We don't want to be hypocrites, so we worry when we don't see the fruits of our beliefs showing in our lives. But the kingdom principle is: We have to believe before we can grow. But once we choose to receive the implanted Word, it begins its work of changing us from the inside—and that work continues whether or not we can see it happening. It may take a while, but the internal change will ultimately be expressed in external behavior. If we judge the seed too quickly, we will abort its sprouting and prevent its fruit.

Betsy later reported that on that night she made a choice to trust in God's declarations regardless of what she could see. When she became a Christian, she had received the truth that Jesus performed everything that God required of us, that he absorbed all the wrath for all her sin—past, present, and future. She had heard the Word that he reconciled her to God and that her full acceptance was not conditioned on her performance. Now she chose to believe that truth afresh and its new ramifications. She was no longer a sinner trying to be righteous, but was now as different from the way she used to be as a tiger is from a tiger lily. This process was happening whether she could see it or not.

Once she received this truth, it began to work inside of her. But again, she didn't see the results immediately. In fact, it was several months later that she realized something had happened. Then she became aware that she was resting more on the inside. The things that used to irritate and harass her no longer bothered her. She was not nearly so preoccupied with judging her performance and the performance of others as she once was. She was noticing the fruit of a previously received Word. Through God's mysterious grace, she was being made holy.

How does sanctification work? We simply don't know. There is something wonderfully mysterious about the process. We can't write books on how it happens. We can't reduce it to a few steps and a simple formula. We must simply receive the Word of God, and let it do its work in us—resisting the temptation to scratch up the seed.

SEEING AND RESPONDING

At the beginning of this chapter I said that sanctification is as simple as hearing and receiving, seeing and responding. We've discussed the importance of hearing; now let's look at seeing.

In an earlier chapter we said that the purpose of the law is to reflect our flaws. It's like a mirror; when we look in it, we see ourselves for what we are. The ultimate purpose of the law is to compel people to run to God. The trouble is, it doesn't always work that way. So many of us, instead, once we've seen ourselves in the law, just keep trying to make ourselves look better. We really think we can do it. We can't.

Jesus is like a mirror, also. But we do not see our weaknesses when we look into his mirror, we see his strengths. And then, amazingly, we start to look like him! That's why it is absolutely essential for believers to keep their eyes focused on the glory of Jesus.

Paul says it like this: "But we all, with unveiled face beholding as in a mirror the glory of the Lord, are being transformed into the same image from glory to glory, just as from the Lord, the Spirit" (2 Cor 3:18). Note the delineation of responsibility given in this statement. What is it that we do, and what is it that God does? It seems clear, according to this statement, that we do the beholding, but God does the transforming.

To me, this Scripture is reminiscent of the time in the wilderness when the children of Israel were being bitten by snakes. (See Numbers 21:4-9.) God said, "If you will put a serpent on the pole and look at the serpent, you will be healed." Now, that doesn't make any sense. There should be no connection between a serpent on a pole and the chemical reaction within a body that has been bitten by a poisonous snake. And yet God said, "If you'll look, you'll live."

Is that too simple? Does that offend the minds of men and women who want to understand how everything works? Do we have to live forever infected by the Tree of the Knowledge of Good and Evil? Or can we, with courage and boldness, step out into the simplicity of beholding the glory of God and allowing that perception to change our lives?

People who are truly looking to Jesus for everything will find that they don't only see Jesus in that mirror; they see themselves *in* Jesus. Everything that Jesus is has been given to us. We are truly heirs of God and joint heirs with Jesus.

Now, gazing on Jesus and allowing him to work in our lives is not the same thing as lying around all day and doing nothing! Remember, Jesus did say "Follow me." As we keep our eyes on him, we must respond to what we see and hear. If we do what we see him do and say what we hear him say, we will be adequately active.

But the point of taking action on the gospel is not to please God or to achieve our own salvation. The reason we need to respond to what we see is that responding helps make what we see a part of us. James says that those who look but don't act tend to go away and forget what they saw. That's how people get into complexity. They look into the perfect law of liberty and see the grace and goodness of God. But because they do not act in response to that grace, they quickly forget what they saw. Then they get involved once more in trying to achieve their own sanctification instead of relying on God to make them holy. No wonder life gets so complicated!

Maybe that's what makes sanctification so tough. It's too simple. It's as simple as hearing the Word of God and receiving it, as seeing the image of God and responding to it. If we add any more than that, we have moved out of New Testament sanctification and into the complexity of religion.

CHAPTER

21 The Simplicity of Hearing God

I HAD JUST FINISHED SPEAKING to a men's group about Jesus' wonderful statement, "I only say what I hear and do what I see." Martin's face revealed that he had not truly enjoyed what I had taught.

"That may sound like good news to you," he said. "But if you heard God as seldom as I do, you wouldn't think so. If I can only do what I see him do and say what I hear him say, I won't be doing or saying much. My life is going to be one boring experience."

I had to admit that Martin had a point. If God only speaks three or four times in a lifetime, then this matter of the Christian life being a response to hearing God is *not* good news. Jesus said, "My sheep hear my voice, and I know them, and they follow me" (Jn 10:27). But what exactly does his voice sound like?

God is light, the Scripture tells us. That means he is self-revealing. He is not trying to hide. It is not God's nature to keep himself from us. Had he wanted to do that, he would never have created us, nor would he have gone to the trouble of sending his own Son to die in order to make communication possible between God and humanity.

God wants to communicate. In fact, he is communicating all the time. And one of the keys to living simple lives instead of drowning in complexities is learning to hear his voice through all the various channels he uses.

THE CREATOR'S VOICE

Romans 1:18-20 indicates that God speaks to us through creation:

> For the wrath of God is revealed... against [those] who suppress the truth in unrighteousness, because that which is known about God is evident within them; for God made it evident to them. *For since the creation of the world his invisible attributes, his eternal power and divine nature, have been clearly seen, being understood through what has been made,* so that they are without excuse. (emphasis added)

So many of the basic truths about God's nature are evident in the world, even to those who have not heard of Jesus. We can learn about God in the orderliness and beauty of the physical world, the poignancy of human need, even the ultimate futility of fleshly life. All these things can be observed by anyone, and they testify to God's greatness. That's why Paul says that even those who are not Christians have no excuse for unrighteousness.

Paul made the same point in Acts 14:15-17. In speaking to Gentiles who were trying to make gods out of him and Barnabas, he pointed out that even those who didn't have the covenant were being spoken to by God through acts of creation.

Creation is not a complete revelation, of course. The whole purpose of this book is to point out that common sense and natural observation are not enough to keep us from living futile lives. And yet creation is a starting point. If we respond to the revelation we find in creation, God will see to it that we get more revelation.

BELIEVE THE WORKS

Sometimes God's voice sounds like his works. The religious people of Jesus' day were having trouble believing that he was truly the Son of God. His encouragement to them was, "If I do not do the works of my Father, do not believe me; but if I do them, though you do not believe me, believe the works, that you may know and understand that the Father is in me, and I in the Father" (Jn 10:37-38). Every miracle Jesus performed was God speaking to those who were watching. Every sign and wonder that ever happened in his earthly ministry was God shouting his nature to those who were listening.

When he healed the sick, he was shouting his mercy. When he fed the hungry, he spoke of his compassion and power. When he walked on the water, he declared his rule over nature. When he raised the dead, he revealed his ultimate victory over death. When he died defenseless for sinners, his unconditional love reverberated throughout the universe.

The sovereign God speaks to us in every event in our lives. God is never reticent to give his revelation to us; he just wants to choose the means through which he communicates. Once we have had our eyes opened to see the glory of God residing in the whole earth, we can receive revelation from him from any source. We realize that he is not limited to any one or two ways of communicating. And because of his permeating influence in all of his creation, he is constantly seeking to let us know what he is really like.

THE OBJECTIVE STANDARD

Sometimes God's voice is heard through searching the Scriptures. Through his written word, God gives us the information we need to be introduced to the living Word. "From childhood you have known the sacred writings which are able to give you the wisdom that leads to salvation through faith which is in Christ Jesus" (2 Tm 3:15).

As we read the Scriptures and become intimate with the God of the Scriptures, we are able to know his character and discern his voice in other ways. The Scriptures are God's eternal, objective standard of revelation. No message that comes to us from God through more subjective means will ever violate the obvious revelation of the written Scriptures.

That's why any person who has a legitimate desire to communicate with God will be a serious student of the holy Scriptures. Without reference to the authority that resides there, subjective communication becomes nothing more than a mumbo-jumbo subjectivism, much like that being set forth by the proponents of the so called "New Age" movement.

THE INNER VOICE

Perhaps the most profound, yet simple, truth about how we can hear God is that God speaks from where he lives. He lives in creation. He lives in history. He has supernaturally preserved the Scriptures for us and lives within their lines. But God has also sent the Holy Spirit to actually dwell within us. Those of us who are going to hear him consistently must learn to hear the inner voice of God.

Remember, we are not living under the old covenant, where God's law is written on an external tablet. Under the new covenant, his law is written on our hearts, so direct communication can continue at all times. To wait for God to speak from some faraway star or to come from some external source is to bypass the most obvious means of communication that God has designed. God talks to us from the inside. Maybe we are so accustomed to being controlled from the outside by manipulation and guilt that we really don't know how to live from the inside out.

I was the youngest child in my family. When I was growing up on the farm, all my brothers and sisters were already grown and had moved away, so I spent a lot of time alone. I played outdoors for hours on end, and sometimes I would talk to God as though he were a friend. I would ask him simple questions like, "What do you think about this?" And then I would tell him what I thought about certain things. And because no one likes one-way conversation, I would not only talk to God with my audible voice, I would use my voice for God to talk back to me. The conversation would go something like this:

"Well, God, what do you really think about me, anyway?"

Then I would speak for God. "Well, Dudley, I really like you. You're really special. I'm going to let you be a part of my work on the earth."

I honestly thought I was making all that up, that I was saying the things I wished God would say if he were speaking to me. The interesting thing is that later on, as I came to know God more intimately, I found out that those same things I used to hear was exactly what God was saying to me through the Scriptures and through the revelation of his Spirit inside of me.

Please note. I'm not saying that we can "put words in God's mouth." What God is saying to us and what we wish he would say are not always the same thing. But I do believe we hear God a lot more than we think we do, and that we can tune our hearts in to his voice.

Not everything that comes out of the heart is of God. But when God speaks to a believer, it does come out of that person's heart—because that's where God lives. And as we grow in him, God promises to renew our hearts, to make us more sensitive to his voice within us: "I will give you a new heart and put a new spirit within you; and I will remove the heart of stone from your flesh and give you a heart of flesh. And I will put my Spirit within you and cause you to walk in my statutes, and you will be careful to observe my ordinances" (Ez 36:26-27).

LIVING OUT OF THE SPIRIT

When we talk about hearing the voice of God, therefore, we're not necessarily talking about some external vision or a special phenomenon. We're talking about responding to the Spirit of God within us.

In Galatians 3 and 4, the apostle Paul is dealing with the change that has come in man's relationship with God. He says that when we are born into the family of God we are no longer slaves, but heirs. And he makes the point that when a child is being brought up under tutors, his or her experience is little different than that of a slave. A child's life is completely controlled by external factors. But as that child grows up and matures, he or she moves into the experience of being an heir, able to operate out of internal desires and knowledge rather than out of external control. When we have received the Spirit of God, we're no longer under an external tutor. We don't have to keep waiting for some external source (such as the law) to tell us what to do.

There is a legitimate time when parents must tell their children the proper things to do. But parents hope one day they will grow up and decide to do some things on their own.

When my son was in his early teens, I gave him the responsibility of maintaining a well-manicured lawn. He was to cut the grass, do the edging and the clipping, and bag up the trash. For this he was to receive an agreed-upon remuneration.

For a long time my son's job took more work on my part than doing it myself would have taken. I had to tell David when it was time to cut the grass, show him how to do it, and also assist in all the repairs needed on the equipment. But I can't tell you the joy I experienced the day that I came home from work and found him out in the yard, cutting the grass, without a single word from me or his mom.

What do you think I did? Do you think I ran out in the yard and chided, "David, who told you to cut this grass? Nobody told you it was time to cut this grass, and it was mighty presumptuous of you to take it on yourself"? You know I didn't. I was thrilled beyond words that my son had obeyed the voice of his heart, rather than just the voice of my mouth.

This is what is so liberating about living under the grace of God. I essentially get to do what my inner person wants to do. No restrictions, no guilt, no condemnation, just living out of the overflow of my spirit. The more I find the true nature of my inner person, the more I find that it wants to do the will of God. Why? Because God's law has been stamped in my heart and in my mind.

In recent years, I have noticed this growing sense of liberty in one of the first areas where I personally learned to hear the specific, directive voice of God in my heart—the area of finances. In the beginning, when I had an opportunity to give, I would ask God exactly how much I was to give. In those early days, I would sense an impression in my spirit to give such specific amounts as fifty-seven dollars and thirty-seven cents instead of a round figure of fifty or sixty dollars. It was interesting to learn to hear God in that way.

These days, however, I have found that God doesn't always speak quite like that. Instead, he seems to let me operate out of my desires. Sometimes I'll have one hundred dollars in my possession and experience a great desire to give it to some particular need. I don't have to wait to get some overt revelation. I just give out of the abundance of my heart, trusting God to let me know if I'm off track.

THE LANGUAGE OF GRACE

All of us are aware that some of the desires that come out of our hearts stem from the flesh rather than the spirit. That's why we must live in honesty before God and dependence on him. And that's why God has been so wonderfully wise in giving us not only the inside revelation stamped in our heart and mind, but the outside revelation of his Scripture. In addition, he has given us the sounding board of friends and fellow believers who are on the same journey of communicating with God.

Once we have tuned our ears to hear the inner voice of God, external confirmations can be very helpful. Personal prophecies, circumstances in which doors are closed or opened, and the advice of others can help us decide whether we have really heard the voice of God.

However, these external confirmations are simply confusing when one is not tuned in to what God is saying on the inside. And to be tuned in to God, we must understand the language he speaks. It can be summed up in these words, "God speaks the language of grace."

When God speaks to his children, he speaks without wrath. His voice to his children was drained of wrath when Jesus died on the cross for our sins; now it is one of unconditional love. That love may have correction and reproof in it, but it will always be loving. The world has nothing to look forward to but wrath. But for God's children, there is only love. If you hear a voice with wrath in it, therefore, it is not the voice of God.

If you're expecting God to speak to you the way your earthly father did, you might miss him altogether. For a long time I was sure that if I ever heard God's voice he would be saying something like this:

"I've been watching you, young man, and you're in serious trouble. I know everything you've done, and every thought you've had. I know more than your parents, and you are worse than anyone knows. If everyone knew what I know about you, you would get no blessings in life and would be locked up forever."

That's what I *expected* God to say. But that's not what he was saying. For he was speaking to me in the context of Jesus' intercessory work for me.

Some time back, I was leading a seminar among couples who wanted to study this subject of hearing God. After we had talked about the concept for awhile, I stopped and gave them a project. "Take a pencil and paper," I told them, and write down this question to God: 'Dear God, what's your opinion of me?' Then I want you to be quiet and write down what you hear as God's answer to you."

I gave the participants fifteen minutes and watched their response. Some began to cry; some began to get really excited; some looked very confused. One of the confused ones came up to me at the break and handed over his paper: "Here's what I heard God say." I read, "You are a total failure. You have never succeeded at anything in your life. You're a failure as a husband; you're a failure as a father; and the fact that you have lost your job means that you're a failure as a man...."

I simply looked at his paper and asked him one question. "Are you truly a Christian?"

He looked confused, but said, "Yes, I am. I know I'm a believer."

"Then," I said, "that is not the voice of God to you. You have heard the voice of accusation, but you have not heard the voice of God. That is not his language."

Now, if you're expecting God to speak like that and instead he is talking to you about his love for you, his plans for you, and his assignments for you, then you will certainly miss him.

DESTINY, NOT HISTORY

Here's something else I have discovered about the voice of God. When he speaks to his children, he speaks on the basis of their destiny, not their history.

Do you remember the story of Gideon? It is found in Judges 6. Gideon was an Israelite. He was the youngest of his family and came from the poorest family of the weakest tribe of Israel. And he lived during a time when Israel was being browbeaten by the Midianites. When Israel's crops were almost ready for harvest, the Midianites would come into the land, burn all the wheat, and ruin everything. When the cows would start to calve, the Midianites would wait until just before they were to give birth and then come in and slaughter the cattle. As a result of these guerrilla tactics, the Israelites had become totally intimidated.

Now, here's the story: Gideon was out one day threshing some wheat, hiding by the winepress so that he would not be spotted by the Midianites. Numb with fear, he tossed the wheat into the air, praying that no one would see him. But only a few yards away, the angel of the Lord was watching this operation. All of a sudden, the air vibrated with the sound of the angel's voice:

"Gideon, you mighty man of valor, the Lord is with you."

Gideon was thinking, "I wonder who he's talking to? I'm from the house of Manasseh, the weakest family in my tribe, and I'm the scaredest kid on the block. I'm trying to get enough wheat so that I won't starve today. I'm scared to death of those Midianites. I'm certainly no mighty man of valor, I'm more like a mighty man of fear."

Gideon was evaluating himself on the basis of his history. But God was speaking to Gideon about his destiny. Gideon probably had the same kind of questions we have: "If the Lord is with me, why are the Midianites winning? If I'm so special to God and he's done all this for me, why am I in so much danger?"

Since the Lord is not limited by time, he could look at the present from the perspective of the future. He knew what he was going to do in Gideon's life. Now Gideon was threshing wheat and cowering with fear. But in a few days Gideon would be routing the Midianites with an undersized army, armed with nothing but pots and candles! The Lord saw that as a completed event, and he spoke to Gideon with victory in view.

This is the way God sees us—and he wants us to see ourselves that way, too.

You remember our favorite character, the apostle Peter? When Jesus first met him, he told Peter who he was and who he was going to become. "You are Simon," Jesus said, "but you will be Peter (a rock)." All through those turbulent three years of training, Jesus loved Peter and knew what Peter would become through him. He looked at Peter through the eyes of destiny.

Paul prayed for his friends in Ephesus: "that the eyes of your heart may be enlightened, so that you may know what is the hope of his calling, what are the riches of the glory of his inheritance" (Eph 1:18). He wanted them to see that they had a higher destiny than they had ever thought about. But he knew it would take a revelation from God for them to see it.

In Philippians 3, Paul wrote of a call that pulled him upward, something that pressed him toward the high calling of Christ in his life. Paul had a sense of destiny. He knew that God had a purpose for him that far exceeded anything his mind could comprehend. He wasn't just going to be a survivalist, afraid of everything around him. Nor was he going to judge himself based on his history. He was pressing onward and upward to obtain the highest God had for him.

If you're expecting God to rehash your past, you're going to miss his voice. He's not talking to you primarily about your history. He's talking to you about your destiny. He's telling you that he has covered your sinful past with the blood of Jesus, and that he chooses to see nothing that is under the blood. He has given you ears to hear his voice from wherever it comes. He is speaking to you all the time through creation, through his works, through his Scriptures, and through the inner voice living inside of you.

He did not put us on earth with only a written manual to live by. Neither does he send us an occasional telegraph to try to keep us in line. God has given us himself. And just as Jesus lived his life in response to his father, we can live our life in response to our shepherd.

He speaks, we move!

PART FIVE

Grace Works

For the grace of God has appeared, bringing salvation to all men, instructing us to deny ungodliness and worldly desires and to live sensibly, righteously and godly in the present age. **Titus 2:11-12**

CHAPTER 22 Addictions and Grace

DOES THE SUBSTANCE of this book have anything to do with life in the pits? Is all this talk about legalism and flesh and simplicity and grace just more theological gobbledygook that priests and preachers spend their time playing with? Well, let's see. In an effort to see if this "life" we've talked about really relates to the average person, let's look at the problem of addictions.

Being addicted is almost as popular these days as having heart surgery was in the eighties. It seems to be a sign of acceptance in the "yuppie" generation not only to have addictions, but to understand one's psychological makeup.

But the fact that addictions are popular doesn't make them any less real—or any less painful. Many of us really do have uncontrollable dependencies that make our lives miserable. Recently I heard a well-known public speaker quote a poll which indicated that 40 percent of Americans struggle with compulsive behavior.

I'll not take the time here to try to give my amateurish psychological dissection of addictions, but simply say that an addiction can be our attempt to medicate a hurt or an attempt to satisfy our eternal longing for real love. Some people attempt to medicate their hurts or satisfy their heart's longing with drugs, some with food, some with fantasies, some with sex, some with work—some even with religion.

Support groups have sprung up all over the country as people are desperately seeking a way to cope with their addictions. And some of these groups, especially the spiritually-based Twelve Step programs, have been invaluable sources of hope and growth. But some people have been going to their support groups for so long that they are even losing hope there, for they have concluded that where once they were addicted to some substance abuse they are now addicted to the support group meetings.

DOES GRACE WORK FOR ADDICTIONS?

The primary question is this: Does the gospel of grace have anything to say about addictions? Does God, through Scripture, give us a workable answer for compulsive behavior, or are we left to ourselves, to struggle around in the quagmire of partial understandings? Can we ever be sure that we can be free from controlling compulsions?

Of course, I believe the answer is yes. God does have a simple, direct word, and it has been given to us through the pages of Scripture. In Romans 6 we find some keys to unlocking the understanding of the addiction problem and the gracious good news about God's decisive cure.

Let me add a caution up front. When I talk about a simple cure for addiction, I don't mean to minimize the pain of those who struggle with compulsive behavior or those who are the victims of others' addictions. Nor do I mean to imply that addictions can be cured overnight just by reading the Bible. (That has been known to happen, but more common is the slow, "one day at a time" recovery.)

I certainly don't want to say that conquering addiction is a "Lone Ranger" problem to be handled just by the addict and God. Although only one person can make the soul-deep decisions of trusting God and his grace, the day-to-day decisions of resisting addictive behavior usually require help. Many people need the encouragement and support of other people in order to face their problem and, with God's help, to grow beyond it. Some may find this in support groups, some in counseling, others simply in fellowship with friends and the body of Christ. Remember, human beings were created for fellowship; we were never meant to face our problems alone. And this is as true in the case of addictions as it is of any other problem we face on earth.

THE SPIRITUAL ORIGINS OF ADDICTION

With that said, let's begin our examination of addictions with a review our humankind's plight and how we got where we are today. God originally created man and woman to enjoy him, to bear his image, and to rule and reign under his authority. From the first, humans were free and well equipped to do all these things. Yet Adam and Even, tempted by the promise of being equal to God, ate of the Tree of the Knowledge of Good and Evil. This choice, in essence, was the choice of independence from God.

As a result of their fateful choice, the first humans suffered the consequences of the Fall, which included immediate self-consciousness. Their eyes fell from beholding the glory of the Lord to beholding their own shame. They were immediately aware that they were not like God, although the Enemy had promised that they would be. Now they were aware that their imperfections were exposed to God. Their shame caused them to hide behind a bush, and humankind has been following their lead ever since.

Self-consciousness is the result of sin. And self-consciousness is a root of addiction. Much compulsive behavior is, in effect, an attempt to cover up our imperfections and shame and hide from the pain of who we are.

The human race was in a terrible mess even before God gave the law to Moses. But the law revealed that humanity's problem was worse than anyone had thought.

Before the law was given, humankind suffered the consequence of sin, which was death... the absence of life. In this death, men and women were self-conscious rather than God-conscious, victims rather than victors. Because they were subject to death, they were well aware that they were ruled over rather than ruling. At the same time, they were not at all aware of the depth of their sin nor the desperate condition of their heart.

When the law was given, a sin-consciousness was added to man's self-consciousness. Thus we have humankind trying to be successful in fulfilling their God-ordained commission, but at the same time laden down with self-consciousness and sin-consciousness. We have suffering and shame passed on from generation to generation; fallenness bringing pain to ourselves and to people who love us.

With this limited perspective, no wonder men and women couldn't find true answers to the human predicament.

GRACE ABOUNDED

Then into the darkness of this pitiful plight came the brightness of the gospel. We will find that it is the nature of grace to always rush toward need: "Where sin increased, grace abounded all the more" (Rom 5:20).

The only thing that grace requires is a need into which to pour itself. Grace is not looking for the independent or the secure, but for the helpless. All that is necessary to qualify for the grace of God is to be needy. (It is at this point that support groups have been invaluable instruments of grace. The atmosphere of acceptance has encouraged many to come out of denial and admit they have a problem.) And certainly a self-conscious, sin-conscious person qualifies for that grace.

One of the most beautiful characteristics of the grace of God is that it is inexhaustible. Even with all your addictions, insecurities, and frailties, you cannot create a need so big that grace cannot meet it. The bigger the hole, the more grace there is to fill it. Even one who has been to God a million times with the same problem need not fear exhausting the grace of God.

Usually it is only arrogance that keeps us from going again and again to God for grace to help in time of need. Sometimes we are talked out of going to God by the Enemy, who tells us, "If you had meant it when you repented, you wouldn't be back for more help." That's a lie! Every time we need grace, we can go to God. And every time we go, we will be strengthened and comforted.

So what answer did God, in his grace, give to our needy human predicament? Significantly, it didn't involve calling us to endless self-examination nor browbeating us with the law. His answer to our pitiful plight was to send his Son. Jesus came to live under the law; to defeat our enemies of sin, Satan, and death through the cross; and to be raised again so that our eyes could be taken off ourselves and put on Jesus.

In other words, the only cure for self-consciousness and sin-consciousness is God-consciousness. The only lasting solution for our human predicament, including addictions, is learning to focus on him and to depend on him.

A NEW KIND OF LIFE

In Romans 6, Paul deals with the natural mind's tendency to misunderstand the grace of God. "What shall we say then? Are we to continue in sin that grace may increase?" (Rom 6:1). Or, "Shall we sin because we are not under law but under grace?" (Rom 6:15). The natural mind thinks, "If grace covers my sin, why not continue so that grace can be magnified?" Its definition of grace would be that grace frees me from the penalty of sin, so I can go satisfy myself with no fear of punishment. This is obviously tempting to those of us who experience the painful compulsion to indulge in addictive behaviors. But such an assumption is a total misunderstanding of the grace of God.

It is true that the grace of God has taken care of eternal judgment, because Jesus became the propitiation for our sins. In doing that Jesus, in himself, absorbed all the wrath that God has for our rebellion. Jesus has left none of the "drippings" of God's wrath for me. "Perfect love casts out fear, because fear involves punishment" (1 Jn 4:18).

But the focus of God's grace is not just on the penalty of my sin, but my bondage to sin on this side of heaven. Grace did not come just to pay my penalty so I could live in the bondage of working sin. It came to set me free from the power of sin and self-consciousness in my own life and even from my bondage to those who have sinned against me.

This is how Paul puts it: "Do you not know that all of us who have been baptized into Christ Jesus have been baptized into his death? Therefore we have been buried with him through baptism into death, in order that as Christ was raised from the dead through the glory of the Father, so we too might walk in newness of life" (Rom 6:3-5).

The Greek word translated "know" in this passage means more than just to be aware of something or to know it theoretically. It means to "know by revelation." Have you noticed that when you know something by revelation, your life changes? You can be aware of an assortment of facts and still experience no change. But God's revelations always change your life.

When Paul says "do you not know?" he is talking about this kind of revelation from God. What is that life-changing revelation? That the grace of God in Jesus made it possible for the old sin-conscious, self-conscious me actually and really to die. What a wonderful thought! I have been buried and raised not only with a new life, but with a new way of viewing life! That's the joy of believing in Jesus and becoming one with him. When I know I have died with Christ, been buried with Christ, and been raised with Christ, I know I am now living in a new kind of life.

This newness of life gives me a new perspective on living. I am no longer sin- and self-conscious, but God-conscious. I am aware of the fact that I have nothing hanging over my head to condemn me. There are no unfulfilled expectations for me. I have been judged in Jesus and found totally pleasing to God the Father. I am free to live my life in union with him, since he has already paid the penalty of my sin and has defeated death itself through his resurrection. He has also fulfilled the law by dying for sin and has defeated Satan through the blood of Jesus on the cross. Because of all this, I stand as a free person with the capability of seeing things differently.

GOOD-BYE TO THE BODY OF SIN

One of the things that happens in this wonderful experience of the cross is that the "body of sin" is done away with (Rom 6:6). What is a "body of sin"? It certainly sounds bad.

It includes that system of deception that we have developed around our addictions. It is based upon the big lie that you require something other than God's life to meet the hurts and unmet needs in your life. It originates from the first lie that Satan told Adam and Eve: "You can be like God by doing something." Ever since that day, human beings have been trying to satisfy their desires and cover their pain with possessions, activities, and experiences. We have the uncanny ability to think rationally and arrive at the wrong conclusions, then to rationalize a course of action that gives us some sort of relief.

The "body of sin" also involves the "big lie" of blame. Addicts are usually expert blamers, attempting to place responsibility for their destructive behavior on everyone but themselves. And it is true that many who develop addictions have been mistreated and sinned against; their pain is real. And yet healing cannot begin until we face squarely the fact that addictive behavior is based on our own choices, thence our own sin. Only in God's grace can we face that painful reality positively.

It is this body of sin that creates and perpetuates the addictions in our lives. We are incomplete apart from God and hurt because of the offenses of this cruel world. So we find medications to satisfy our longing for completion. But we will always have hurts that are not comforted, wounds that are not healed, and needs that are not met until we come into union with Jesus Christ himself. And when he comes again in glory, this union will be made perfect and full. It is in Christ and Christ alone that we can enjoy God, bear his image, and rule under his authority. That is God's success. Everything else leaves us dissatisfied and unfulfilled.

CHOOSING YOUR MASTER

There is no ultimate cure for our hidden or not-so-hidden addictions, apart from a personal experience of the cross—that is, a personal experience of being joined with Jesus in his death, burial, and resurrection. When that experience happens to us, then we truly have died to one perspective and been raised to another by the Spirit of God that dwells in us. And then our freedom really does become possible.

In giving us freedom, however, God does not take away our choices. Free human beings can even choose to put themselves back into bondage. That's why the latter part of Romans 6 deals with this matter of choosing who will be your master. Romans 6:14-23, as I understand it, tells us this: Before grace came into your lives you were slaves to sin. Since the grace of God has been revealed, you are slaves to righteousness. The great news is this: When you became slaves to righteousness, you no longer were obligated to obey your old master, sin. Now you have the capacity to obey righteousness and when you do, you will be fulfilled.

These verses also talk about the principle of establishing authority in your life. Basically, Paul says you have the right to establish who or what has authority in your life. If you yield yourself to someone; you establish that person as your authority (my paraphrase).

Have you ever watched any of the old Westerns where the gangsters were mean, dirty, derelict, and yet were controlled by their mother? She's always a spindly little old lady. And there's always a scene where they are in their cabin in the badlands of Mexico, having just returned from robbing a bank and killing a few poor souls. These mean desperadoes come in to eat, spitting and putting their elbows on the table and acting unmannerly. Inevitably "Ma" grabs one of them by the ear and makes him shut up and sit down. It is obvious that she rules the clan. These are men that cannot be controlled by laws. The best Texas rangers and the finest marshals that ever pinned on a star cannot control them. Yet this little woman rules them easily. Why? Because when they were young they yielded to her as their authority. They gave her authority in their lives, and they can't get over it.

This is what happens to us in our addictions. When we continue to yield to an authority in our life, each time we yield we establish that authority on a higher level. But the answer to being free from some negative authority is not to focus on escaping that authority, but to realize that, in the kingdom of God, we already have a higher master.

When we made a choice years ago, months ago, or even days ago, to be united with Jesus in death, burial, and resurrection, we established him as the authority. Because of that, we can daily choose to yield to righteousness and to establish righteousness as an authority in our lives. In a sense, we can become addicted to righteousness. And that is the only long-term cure to being addicted to substances or food or other people or any other undependable source of satisfaction.

What a wonderful thought! The key is not to focus on saying no to the temptation of evil, but to saying yes to the temptation of good!

Notice the phrases in Romans 6:19: "just as" and "so now." The verse says, in essence, "*Just as* you were slaves of unrighteousness you would yield your members one step at a time, developing higher degrees of unrighteousness, *so now,* yield your members one step at a time, developing higher degrees of righteousness" (my paraphrase).

That's the key. Yielding to righteousness, not saying no to unrighteousness. It's true that when you say yes to righteousness you will be saying no to unrighteousness. But the key is the focus. Do you see? Every time there is a temptation to yield to that false god that was promising a satisfaction for your deep yearnings, you can say yes to Jesus, who has taken your old life with him in death and resurrection. The authority of the old system of deception has been usurped by a higher authority. You are no longer defined by your addictions to alcohol, food, work, or other people. You are free from their authority. You are forgiven. You are a child of God.

As a free child of God, you may choose to become involved in any activity you want. But you *do* have the choice. You can reckon yourself to be dead to sin but alive unto God and choose to say yes to righteousness every time there's a temptation.

YOU CAN ALWAYS BEGIN AGAIN

Now the question arises, "What if I fail? What if I yielded to the temptation of evil rather than to the temptation of good?" The moment you recognize you've done so, step out from behind Adam's bush and say to God, "I've chosen the wrong way." (It helps to say that to another human being, too.) Every time you confess and determine to make better choices the next time, you are choosing the right way. Every time you confess, you're establishing righteousness as an authority in your life.

You say, "But what if I do it a hundred times? Doesn't that mean that I really didn't mean it when I repented?"

No, it doesn't. It means that you are still trusting the inexhaustible grace of God. And every time you confess and repent, you reestablish righteousness in your life.

You say, "Do you think I will ever stop my destructive behavior?"

Yes, because God desires not only to free you from the *penalty* of sin but to free you from the *power* of sin. That's why it is foolish to believe you can be a partaker of grace and continue on nonchalantly in a life of ungodliness.

Grace doesn't just change your destiny, it changes your identity. You're no longer a slave to unrighteousness, but a slave to righteousness. Every chance you get to obey, to submit to Christ, do it. For in this you are establishing righteousness in your life. Then, when you look in the mirror, you will not be tempted to judge yourself by your history but you can, with sincerity of heart, agree with God and judge yourself by your destiny. You are one of God's children, addicted to righteousness!

CHAPTER

23 Living from the Inside Out

THE WHOLE FAMILY SITS IN GLOOM—Dad with his hand on his chin, Mom with worried fear in her eyes, and Rachel, swinging her crossed leg, chewing her gum, and looking aimlessly at the ceiling. The family has reached a communication impasse. Mom and Dad think it reasonable for a fifteen-year-old to have a curfew. They also want to have some say about whom Rachel goes out with. Rachel's response has been to run away from home. She doesn't want a life of rules, she says. She thinks she should be allowed to do what she wants, when she wants, and to be free at last from all restrictions.

So what's the problem here? We have two value systems clashing. Mom and Dad want to protect Rachel from harm and guide her into adulthood with its accompanying responsibilities and freedom. Rachel thinks they just want to cramp her style. She values her "freedom" above everything—and her definition of freedom is "no rules."

This family problem is much like the one our heavenly Father has. Many of his children focus on the rules themselves rather than the values of the Father who placed them there. They see Christian disciplines as edicts to live by or laws for self-improvement. Thinking God has designed these rules to bring unhappiness and restriction, these narrow-minded children rebel.

A QUESTION OF MOTIVATION

Have you ever wondered why so many of us have such little motivation to observe the disciplines of the Christian life?

When I'm speaking to a group of people about this subject, I commonly ask them to list what they consider to be the three most important disciplines of the Christian life. I also ask them to grade their performance in these areas on a scale of one to ten.

When the tests are in, the disciplines listed always include things like prayer, Bible study, fasting, loving one another, attending church, tithing, or giving to the poor. The average grade is somewhere between one and four.

Then I ask them to answer this simple question: "Why don't you observe these disciplines?" The answer can usually be answered succinctly: "I'm not motivated enough."

But where does motivation come from?

When my son lived at home, one of my his domestic chores was to take out the garbage every Monday and Wednesday morning and bring the garbage cans back to the garage after they had been emptied. This is not a monumental task. The time it takes is somewhere between thirty seconds and two minutes. Garbage is not all that heavy and, because we use plastic bags and ties, not all that smelly. And yet David had a constant problem remembering to take out the garbage and bring in the containers.

Now, this boy possessed a decent level of intelligence. He graduated valedictorian of his class, so I'm fairly sure he is not brain dead. In other activities he has shown great diligence and the ability to remember things of importance. He played basketball on his high school team and never forgot a practice or a game. I've actually watched him run sprints until his body was so fatigued he could hardly walk.

Why was he able to perform such difficult tasks as playing basketball and was unable to perform such menial tasks as taking out the garbage and bringing in the containers? The answer, of course, is motivation.

I have a beautiful teenaged daughter, Karis. Many times she will come home from school very tired from the activities of the day. She's not only participated in her scholastic activities, but been to the gym for her workout. As she walks in the door, she drops her books and her sweater and stumbles toward the staircase, mumbling, "I'm so tired I can't study; I can't even talk."

When she is halfway up the stairs, however, the phone rings. It is sixteen-year-old Jason, allegedly calling about a homework assignment. In a matter of seconds, Karis is animated and giggling, talking on the phone. Only a few minutes before she was so tired she couldn't even say "good evening." But when she put that phone to her ear, energy began to flow through her body. She is completely reenergized.

What's the issue? Once again, it's motivation.

We might as well face it. The hope of something gained is a great motivator in all our activities. We are motivated by looking for a payout. And God doesn't seem to mind offering a "payout" to those who follow him. The question is, what payout are we looking for? Many people are disenchanted with the disciplined Christian life. Someone has accurately defined disenchantment as looking for the wrong payout at the wrong time from the wrong places for the wrong reasons. It makes sense, then, to examine our motivations for living "the Christian life." Exactly what reward are we expecting?

God often begins the process of reaching us by appealing to our motive to survive. The first declaration of the gospel that many hear is, "Flee from the wrath to come." This motive to survive is what most often causes people to look toward God to prevent their destruction.

Once we turn to him, however, God begins the process of

moving us to higher levels of motivation until we reach the point that we have chosen his values as ours. It is only at that point that we become free. God's values become our values. And we are motivated to act, to follow Christian disciplines—not because we fear retribution, but because we value the results of these specific actions.

GOD'S VALUE SYSTEM

So now the question becomes, "What are God's values?" Jesus made the answer to that very clear when he responded to the lawyer's question, "Teacher, which is the great commandment in the Law?" Jesus said to him, "'You shall love the Lord your God with all your heart, and with all your soul, and with all your mind.' This is the great and foremost commandment. The second is like it, 'You shall love your neighbor as yourself.' On these two commandments depend the whole Law and the Prophets" (Mt 22:37-40).

Jesus established once and for all that God's greatest value is placed on relationships.

All our lives we have been taught, directly and indirectly, that our greatest value is performing well—that we are judged by what we do. But God has established a new value system. And God has told us that when we adopt that value system, we will appreciate relationships more than anything else in our existence.

The most valuable relationship of all, of course, is a relationship with God. In fact, the highest gain or reward that God could offer to us human beings is the privilege of knowing him. (See Philippians 3:8-10).

Think of it. The possibility that finite, limited me might know the infinite, unlimited God! Actually *know* him! That I might be not only his friend, but his child. And not only his child, but his heir. Not only his heir, but his co-worker in this world. What a reward! What a hope! What a value to be chosen!

Can't you see that when we really adopt this value, it will directly affect all the decisions and choices of our lifestyle? Surely the person whose one goal in life is to know God will spend time reading the book God has written and spend time talking with him in undistracted prayer. Such a person will also spend time relating to Christ's body, the church. He or she will love those people the Father loves.

Christian disciplines grow innately out of our lives once we have adopted the same values as God himself. Our whole perspective shifts. We begin to see righteousness in terms of anything that builds up our relationships with God and God's children. We understand ungodliness in terms of activity that denigrates or undervalues relationships.

I visited a friend of mine who had been at the point of death for three months. He had recovered enough to talk, and when I visited him, he whispered, "Dudley, I've been to death's door again, and I came back to tell you that the only two things in life that are worth anything are Jesus and your friends. And you're my friend."

I was both honored and enlightened by his remark. His remark has also encouraged me to simplify my lifestyle. I realize I must remove any activity or possession that hinders my relationship with God or with people.

COMFORTED, NOT COMFORTABLE

There's another value that may shock you in the way I state it. It seems that we humans will invariably value comfort when given the choice. It is interesting to me that we take all the technological advances of this age and use them to make our lives easier, more comfortable. God's value, however, is not our being *comfortable*, but our being *comforted.*

Many Christians seem to define the victorious Christian life as a "hassle free" life. God, on the other hand, defines the Christian life as one of intimacy with the Holy Spirit whose name is "the Comforter" or "the Helper." (See John 14:16, 26.)

In 2 Corinthians 1:3, we are told that God allows us to have affliction so he can pour the comfort of the Holy Spirit into that affliction. As a result, we can take the comfort we've received and give it to others in their affliction. It is not God's design that we live our entire life without any problems, afflictions, or pain. It *is* his design, however, to fill those problems, afflictions, or pain with an overabundance of his comfort so that we will not only sympathize with others who are going through the same trials, but have an abundance of grace and divine life to share with them.

When my father was teaching me how to swim, I remember being afraid of the deep water. His advice to me was very sound: "Son, it doesn't matter how deep the water is if you stay on top." The apostle Peter, after his experience of walking on the water, sinking, and then being carried by Jesus received even better advice: "It doesn't matter how deep the water is if you are walking on top of it with Jesus."

JOY IS ALWAYS WORTH THE PRICE

The truth is, it doesn't matter how many problems and afflictions we have in life if there is adequate comfort of the Holy Spirit to meet our need. Our goal, therefore, should not be to make it through life without any problems, but to remain open to God's grace. He has given us the Holy Spirit to live in us and turn our weaknesses into his strengths. This life of being comforted by the Holy Spirit is truly the joyful life that Jesus came to bring. It is worth whatever it costs to have it.

Jesus told the story about a man who found a pearl of great price. He sold all that he had because of the surpassing value of the pearl (Mt 13:45-46). It is when we see the surpassing value of the joyful life that we become willing to forfeit anything in our lives that is keeping us from possessing it.

Most of us have a lot to give up. We must rid ourselves of the guilt we have carried unnecessarily. We must shrug off the regret of our past failures. We must forfeit the fear that has paralyzed us. We must put away the pet doctrines that have given us false identities. We must realign our schedules that keep us so busy that we don't have time to focus on true values.

Such forfeitures are not always easy because making God's values our values is an ongoing process, not completed in this lifetime. Giving up the things that hold us back from comfort can be downright uncomfortable! But payoff is always worth the price. The joyful life is worth whatever it costs to have it.

We are actually illustrating the real nature of repentance here. In the kingdom of God, repentance is a matter of trading up. It is, in essence, a matter of seeing a value greater than anything we have had before and then ridding ourselves of anything that keeps us from having it.

GETTING WHAT YOU DON'T DESERVE

The joyful life of intimacy with God and comfort from the Holy Spirit is the life of grace. It cannot be achieved, earned, or developed. If it is to be experienced, it must be received. Herein lies the biggest problem to the whole grace question. Those of us who have been trained in the "You only get what you deserve" mentality have a difficult time receiving what we don't deserve and can't earn.

Several years ago I was selling a used mobile home. The man who had come to appraise its value found a Western hat I had left hanging in the closet. I could tell he was very enamored of that hat.

Finally he asked, "What would you take for that hat?"

"Do you like it?" I asked in reply.

"Yes," he said, "I've always wanted a hat like that."

"Does it fit?" I asked.

After trying it on, he decided it fit very nicely.

"What would you take for it?" he asked again.

"Oh," I said, "I'll just give it to you."

"No-o-o-o," he demurred, "I couldn't do that. I'll be happy to pay you for it."

"No," I said, "it's fine. I would like to give you the hat."

"Oh, no," he protested. "I couldn't do that. What do you want for it?"

"I don't want anything for it," I said. "I would like to give you the hat."

"Oh, no. I just wouldn't feel right about that."

Finally, I looked at him and said, "This is my hat. It's paid for. I don't owe anything on it, and I can do with my hat whatever I choose. If you ever get this hat, you'll have to receive it as a gift from me."

I shall never forget his response. He actually turned his back to me, stuck his hand out to the side, and mumbled, "Okay, but I'd rather pay for it."

As I walked away from that experience, I almost heard the heavens mumble as my heavenly Father spoke to me and said, "That's the way you look to me when I try to give you my grace."

It is truly a humbling experience to receive what we don't deserve and can't earn. And yet that's the kind of gift God's grace is. And if we are ever to possess it, we must receive it by faith. We cannot ever do enough to deserve it.

In fact, a vital part of the repentance process is getting rid of that old mentality that still believes we can get something on the basis of our merit. All of that mentality must be sold, destroyed, gotten rid of forever if we're going to embrace the reality of the joyous life of relationship and the comfort of the Holy Spirit.

Yes, we must give up a lot for Jesus… everything that stops the flow of God's grace in our lives. But that's not bad news! That's *good news*! God has given us a life that has his values built into it!

A BUILT-IN RIGHTEOUSNESS

But that's not all the good news. Not only do we have the liberating possibility of having the same values as our Father, we also have the liberty of knowing that those values have been written in our hearts. That's right. We don't have to go to some external source to discover what God's values are. Because of his grace, they are inscribed on our insides. So you see, God has actually made it possible for those of us who have adopted God's values as his own to live as he wants to live.

I will make a prediction. When you discover the depth of your own heart as a believer, you will discover that your values are the same as God's. In other words, what you want and what he wants are the same. And that means you can live your life getting what you really want. You won't have to live your life focused on "rules"—and yet you will find yourself conforming to the character qualities that God values so highly.

To understand more fully what I'm talking about, let's look at a passage of Scripture that has caused great consternation for many through the years, Psalm 15:

> O Lord, who may abide in thy tent?
> Who may dwell on thy holy hill?
> He who walks with integrity, and works righteousness,
> and speaks truth in his heart.
> He does not slander with his tongue,
> nor does evil to his neighbor,
> nor takes up a reproach against his friend;
> In whose eyes a reprobate is despised,
> But who honors those who fear the Lord;
> He swears to his own hurt, and does not change;
> He does not put out his money at interest,
> Nor does he take a bribe against the innocent.
> He who does these things will never be shaken.

For many, this seems to be an almost impossible list of required achievements. If that's what we must do in order to live in the presence of Holy God, why bother trying? Who can do it? And even if we try, who can know when we walk in enough integrity, work enough righteousness, speak with total truth, and so on?

But watch how this passage is transformed into loveliness when we look at it in terms of choosing God's values and having those values written on our heart. When intimacy with God and relationships with others become the most important value in our lives:

- We are able to walk in integrity, because we are walking in accordance with the way we are, not according to some external standard.
- We are able to work righteousness, because righteousness is a matter of managing our relationships, not conforming our lives to an external code.
- We are able to speak truth in our hearts, because untruth will damage those relationships we value so highly.
- We won't slander our neighbor, because he or she is important.
- We won't take up reproach against our friends, because our friends are our most valuable treasure on earth. We will honor those who fear the Lord because they are in our family and our relationships are important.
- We are willing to "swear to our own hurt"—keeping our word even if it inconveniences us—because we value other people's priorities as much as our own.
- We handle our money properly, not using it to the detriment of others, because relationships are infinitely more valuable than money is.

Do you see how internalizing the values of God will affect your choices, but will also take your focus off rules? As a result, all the pressure is off. When his values are inscribed in our hearts, we lead a godly life, but we lead it from the inside out.

Isn't it wonderful what God has done in his grace? He not only has taken care of our past through the blood of Jesus and taken care of our future through the promise of eternal life. He has also given himself—and in giving himself he has given us his values. He has set us free to live according to the dictates of our spirit, knowing that when we do so we will live according to his values. For he has written his law in our hearts and in our minds.

This life truly is a pearl of great price. It's worth selling everything we have to obtain. And one of the main things we have to sell is the belief that we can buy it with anything but faith.

That's just the way grace works.